The Power of an Open Question

The Power of an Open Question

The Buddha's Path to Freedom

Elizabeth Mattis Namgyel

Foreword by Dzigar Kongtrül

SHAMBHALA
Boulder
2011

Shambhala Publications, Inc.
4720 Walnut Street
Boulder, Colorado 80301
www.shambhala.com

9 8 7 6 5 4

Printed in the United States of America

⊗This edition is printed on acid-free paper that meets the American
National Standards Institute z39.48 Standard.
♻Shambhala Publications makes every effort to print on recycled paper.
For more information please visit www.shambhala.com.

Shambhala Publications is distributed worldwide by Penguin Random
House, Inc., and its subsidiaries.

Designed by Daniel Urban-Brown

The Library of Congress catalogues the hardcover edition of this book as
follows:
Mattis-Namgyel, Elizabeth.
The power of an open question: the Buddha's path to freedom / Elizabeth
Mattis-Namgyel; foreword by Dzigar Kongtrül.—1st ed.
p. cm.
Includes bibliographical references.
ISBN 978-1-59030-799-1 (hardcover: alk. paper)
ISBN 978-1-59030-927-8 (pbk.: alk. paper)
1. Religious life—Buddhism. 2. Uncertainty—Religious aspects—
Buddhism. I. Title.
BQ5405.M39 2010
294.3'444—DC22
2010021104

In the spirit of the Mahayana Buddhadharma,
I dedicate this book to all living beings.
May the hearts and minds of all beings rest at ease.
And may they abide in the confidence
of the Middle Way of being.

Contents

Foreword

Elizabeth and I met in Nepal. We were very young, deeply in love, and learning about life, as well as learning how to integrate the Buddhadharma into our lives. I was in the privileged position of knowing more about the Buddhist teachings, having had exposure to the study and practice of Dharma with many great masters of our time. I was able to share that with Elizabeth, and she became my first Dharma student.

Over the many years of our life together, which included coming to the West, raising our son, and starting Mangala Shri Bhuti, our Dharma community, we made an effort to be true to ourselves in the vision of the Dharma, amid a worldly life. In keeping with these principles, Elizabeth was able to do an immense amount of study of the classical texts of Indian and Tibetan philosophy. While in school, she would rise at four o'clock every morning in order to have a full session of practice before the family awoke. Later, when we moved to Crestone, Colorado, she began seven years of intensive practice, at her retreat cabin in the mountains near the family home. Throughout this time, she continued to contribute to our community by serving as an example and guiding students in retreat. Her dedication to study and practice has paved the way for many others to move forward on their paths.

In recent years I've encouraged Elizabeth to step up and become a teacher of our lineage, and for whomever seeks her guidance. I suggested that it would be wonderful if she were to write a book, because Buddhism in the West needs to be established by Western teachers who are able to fully embody the wisdom of the lineage and the teachings. Elizabeth has put her heart and soul into bringing the teachings to life in her own experience, and I feel now is the right and auspicious time for Elizabeth to step forward as a teacher. I'm so glad that she is traveling around to teach and that this book has come to be.

Her book captures all that she has learned about the Buddhadharma, without watering down the meaning. She makes clear how relevant the teachings are to one's own transformation, and I'm confident that others will be able to easily relate this to their own experience. I've read *The Power of an Open Question* thoroughly, and I highly value its essence and the meaningful effect I can foresee it having on others.

Dzigar Kongtrül Rinpoche
August 26, 2009

Acknowledgments

I received my first introduction to the teachings on emptiness from my teacher and husband, Dzigar Kongtrül Rinpoche. I was young then. I don't think I understood exactly what he was getting at. But he didn't let up. Over the years, Rinpoche has continued to teach me with patience, tenderness, urgency, and a lot of fierceness, too. I think he did so simply out of his love for these teachings and out of his kindness, because he knows the transformative effect they can have on others. Now I love them, too. The teachings on emptiness, also known as the Mother of Transcendent Wisdom* or the Middle Way, have always been closest to my heart. They have changed the way I look at life. I spend much of my day grappling with them, pondering them, and delighting in them. How can I ever repay my teacher's kindness?

When Rinpoche asked me to write this book, Sasha Meyerowitz got on board. The profundity of these teachings pulled him in as

*Prajnaparamita (Sanskrit).

well, and he has spent hours with me musing about emptiness and how to express it. What could be more enjoyable than discussing the Buddhadharma with a Dharma friend?

There are many others to thank. So many readers jumped in and came to my aid, all of them seduced by the teachings of the Mother of Emptiness, Prajnaparamita herself. Among them are my beloved son, Jampal Norbu, a friend and support to me since the day he was born. Many thanks to my Dharma companions Gretchen Kahre-Holland, Chris Holland, Mark Kram, Erica Hennigan, and Larry Shainberg for their valuable and thoughtful suggestions. And thank you to Greg Seton for enthusiastically sending me transliterations and translations of words in the midst of his heavy workload.

Ani Pema Chödrön shared her sharp insights. In fact, I created a couple of new chapters, thanks to her. And my mom, Naomi Mattis, *does* always know best. My brother, Chime Mattis, helped me simplify. "Say it in the simplest way possible" was his motto. And my dad, Marvin Mattis . . . well, you see him in this book a lot. He always plays the devil's advocate, drawing out clarity I didn't know I had.

There are others who also just magically showed up in my life and supported me in ways they probably don't even know: with deep gratitude I thank Buddy Frank, Tatjana Krizmanic, and Linda Webber.

And then there are my four-legged friends: the horse Braeburn and the cat Don Julio.

Last but not least I want to express my appreciation for my friends at Shambhala Publications: Emily Bower, Jonathan Green, Hazel Bercholz, Peter Turner, Jim Zaccaria, Ben Gleason, and the copy editor, Gretchen Gordon. It is always a pleasure.

In truth, when working with teachings of such profundity, everything you encounter supports your endeavor; everything falls into place. I appreciate everyone and all of it. Writing this book was pure joy.

The Power of an Open Question

Introduction

Colorado has a lot of rocks, and people like to climb them. Everywhere you go in Colorado you see people on rocks—big rocks. I always wondered how they could climb something so vertical. Not long ago, my friend took me climbing for the first time, and I found out for myself.

It amazed me to see how rock-climbing forces you to do so much with so little. It forces you to pay attention to shallow patterns and textures in the rock you wouldn't ordinarily notice. You make your way up the face of a rock by anchoring parts of your body into these spaces; you push into them, pull against them, and balance on them. When I watch experienced climbers, I'm stunned by what they can do. But this is beside the point. What really captivates me about climbing and what I want to talk about here is the experience of being suspended on a rock and not seeing any possibilities for moving up or down.

Hanging off a rock is an exaggerated experience of facing the unknown. It is exhilarating, scary, and completely vibrant. When we can't find a foothold, the mind falls into an open stillness—the same open stillness we encounter in any situation in which we lose our familiar reference points. If we have the wherewithal to relax, we find our way. But the ordinary reactive mind panics in these moments. Our body tightens, our breath shortens, our vision narrows. All our sense perceptions and our ability to reason are stifled. After a while, muscle strain stirs our sensibilities: "I can't stay like this forever." We don't have the luxury of avoidance, so we work with our fear and slowly we soften. Now, this is the fascinating part: as we soften, we notice all kinds of new patterns and shapes emerging from the rock. We see places to balance we didn't see before. We're not doomed after all. As we soften and open, we access a special intelligence, unimpeded by habitual, reactive mind.

The state of not-knowing is a riveting place to be. And we don't have to climb rocks to experience it. For instance, we encounter not-knowing when we meet someone new or when life throws us a surprise. These experiences remind us that change and unpredictability are the pulse of our very existence. No one really knows what will happen from one moment to the next: who will we be, what will we face, and how will we respond to what we encounter? We don't know, but there's a good chance we will encounter some rough, unwanted experiences, some surprises beyond our imaginings, and some expected things, too. And we can decide to stay present for all of it.

When we decide to stay present for all of it, we enter the spiritual path. Any spiritual path should provide us with an understanding that gradually leads us beyond habitual, reactive mind so that we can engage life with intelligence and openness. Aside from this, what could a path do for us other than encourage our usual attempt to create a semblance of security, but with a spiritual face? Nothing would change. We would continue to shrink from the unknown and chase after the familiar in our habitual effort to recreate ourselves. We might even convince ourselves that we won't have to participate in the unpredictability of life—a fact we can't truly escape from.

The Buddhist Lojong,* or mind-training tradition, says: "Don't be so predictable." As spiritual practitioners, we need to have some curiosity about the unknown. When unexplored territory frightens us, we might ask ourselves, "Where's my sense of adventure?" It's important to have a sense of adventure in life, because our very situation is not unlike climbing up that rock.

THE DECISIVE MOMENT

The way we respond to the stream of momentary experiences we call "our life" determines our move toward our habitual search for security or toward awakening. The Buddhist tradition has many ways of explaining our tendencies to shrink from experience, but all these explanations have one thing in common: pain and suffering proliferate when we can't stay present with what we encounter. When we get overwhelmed by the rich energy of experience we put a lid on it, try to consume it, embellish it, or react to it in one way or another.

The Buddhist Abhidharma† tradition uses a poignant image of an old blind woman to illustrate this decisive moment. Her blindness symbolizes that the truth overwhelms her. In fact, this blindness, or ignorance, serves as her means of escape from resting naturally in the open fullness of experience. Does this tendency have a beginning? We can't say. But this example indicates that we can recognize this tendency in each moment of our lives and know that we have a choice.

---

*The Lojong (Tibetan, Blo sbyong), or mind-training tradition, is based on a set of fifty-nine proverbs that represent the wisdom of the Buddhist Mahayana. These teachings were formulated in Tibet by Geshe Chekawa in the twelfth century. Their purpose, when meditated upon, is to undermine the habitual tendencies that arise from clinging to the self, to cultivate compassion, and to develop insight into the empty nature of phenomena.

†The Sanskrit term *Abhidharma* (Tibetan, Chos mngon pa) is often translated as "higher knowledge," "inner science," or "special knowledge." The knowledge of the Abhidharma is "special" in that it breaks down all experience—everything to be known—in a clear and

Unless we engage situations that challenge habitual mind, such as meditation practice and retreats where most of our usual distractions aren't present, we often don't experience this choice. My friend Rosemary went into her first retreat many years ago. The minute she entered her cabin, the prospect of facing the rawness of her undistracted mind posed an excruciating threat. She bolted out the door and just started running. As she ran deeper into the woods and farther from her cabin, a question arose: "Where can I possibly go?" Unable to answer, she went back to her cabin. Thus began her venture into the exploration of mind, the unknown, and the rest.

To see that we have a choice either to stay present or to run is a powerful thing. It gives us the option of reclaiming our life, which means responding intelligently to what we encounter. What would happen if, while suspended on that rock, we made a conscious choice to rest in open stillness instead of panicking? What would happen if, like Rosemary, we went back to our cabin to sit?

The example of the old blind woman raises an important question: if our struggle finds its genesis in our habit of turning away from the open state, what would happen if we habituated ourselves to staying open?

PAINT AND AN OPEN CANVAS

The fact that nothing is certain, and we therefore can't hold on to anything, can evoke fear and depression in the mind. But it can also evoke a sense of wonder, curiosity, and freedom. In fact, some of our best moments come when we haven't yet decided what will happen next: riding a horse, the wind in our hair; on a bike,

---

distinct way. This ancient literature (third century B.C.E. and later) presents a collection of systematic lists, sequences, and processes related to the Buddha's fundamental psychological model of the mind and the phenomena it perceives. Its central themes include states of consciousness, mental factors, the functions of the mind, the material world, dependent arising, and the methods and stages of meditation.

nothing but open road ahead; traveling in a foreign land where we've never been before. Paint and an open canvas. A typewriter and an empty sheet of paper. Falling in love. When we watch one of those "spaghetti western" films starring Clint Eastwood, we see him wandering through the world, nowhere in particular to go, alone. Anything can happen—we don't know what—but we don't mind; we know he can handle it. We feel attracted to this kind of confidence, this freedom of movement, this way of mingling with the world and its romantic loneliness.

What will we encounter next: coming together, separation, loss, surprise? My father told me that the moment I was born he was overtaken by a mixture of amazement, hope, and trepidation. He wondered, "What is to become of her . . . ?" My son is in his twenties and I still feel wonder, excitement, and heartbreak as I watch him grow into his life. Try to find a parent who doesn't feel this way. How curious that love and uncertainty come together.

Life is full. In fact, life is so touching, curious, sad, exciting, scary, and bittersweet it's almost unbearable at times. But as human beings, we need to ask ourselves: "Must we turn away from life's fullness?" To turn or not to turn—to stay open—this is the question. And this kind of questioning takes us deep into the heart of personal inquiry and shows us how to fully embrace our humanity.

I

A Personal Koan

I have a personal koan.*

> "How do we live a life we can't hold on to?" How do
> we live with the fact that the moment we're born we
> move closer to death; when we fall in love we sign up for
> grief? How do we reconcile that gain always ends in loss;
> gathering, in separation?

I don't know if my question will ever find an answer. But I see
it as a question to live by. I've always felt that if you have a genuine
question you should explore it. All you have to do is continue to
ask it and pay attention.

*In the Buddhist Zen tradition a koan is a paradoxical story, statement, question, or dialogue
that is inaccessible to conventional thought. The practitioner uses the koan as a starting
point for meditative inquiry. By focusing on a single question he or she seeks a way of being
that transcends ordinary answers or solutions. This transcendence is similar to the mind of
an open question: a mind that is engaged yet does not search for security or conclusions.

I feel lucky. I have an amazing example and guide, someone who supports me in the exploration of my koan: the Buddha.

The Buddha had the same question I have. He wanted to find a way beyond basic human suffering—the suffering of birth, old age, sickness, and death. That any one of us may have the same question as the Buddha is not surprising. It's basically the human dilemma. If his question had nothing to do with the human dilemma his teachings wouldn't be of much use to us. But the Buddha was driven by this question, and it guided him to an extraordinary discovery that speaks directly to our experience.

Unfortunately we can't just hijack his discovery; nothing replaces direct experience. Koans are a personal matter. No one else can experience our mind or answer our own questions. Nonetheless, the way the Buddha lived his life and the questions that he asked can inspire and guide us in the direction of wisdom. One of the most provocative things about his awakening was the way he arrived at it—the way he asked his question.

THE UNRELIABLE NATURE OF THINGS

The story of the Buddha's search for truth was marked by two phases of his young life: a disenchantment with ordinary, worldly existence and his encounter with asceticism.

The Buddha was born in India as the son of a king. While the Buddha was still an infant, an old sage visited the palace. He prophesied that the Prince would either become a great ruler or renounce worldly life to seek a liberation that would strike at the very core of human suffering. As the Prince matured he did indeed ask big questions about life and the suffering of the human condition. He had a natural predilection for the truth.

Concerned that he might one day lose his son to a life of spiritual pursuit, the king attempted to distract the boy away from his inquiry by steering him toward the politics of the palace. He tried to entice him with beautiful women, food, and entertainment. But nothing soothed the mind of the Prince. He knew that political power and wealth couldn't protect him from uncertainty, old age, sickness, and death. He felt the vulnerability of his own humanity. He felt the vulnerability of the human condition—the same vulnerability we all feel. But instead of running from it, instead of trying to create a false semblance of security, he probed even deeper. The seductions of the palace didn't capture him. He had the spirit of wanting to know. He was relentless in his search for a truth that would break open the mysteries of human suffering and provide a path of liberation for all living beings. So he left.

The Buddha left because he saw the unreliable nature of things. Although we may not be conscious of it, we hold a lot of assumptions about the nature of things. By "things," we refer here to all the elements that make up our experience: the physical or tangible world, emotional and physical feelings, the information we receive through our senses, our thoughts, and consciousness.

One of these assumptions is that things possess innate qualities that can make us happy and save us from uncertainty, loneliness, and fear. If only we had more power and influence, we would be happy. If we had a relationship, we wouldn't feel so lonely. If we had more money or beauty, we wouldn't feel so insecure. Individually, we each have the tendency to seek a comfortable state of self-deception. Society offers us the promise of security: you need this, you need that; hey, look over here; this will make you bigger, this will make you smaller; this will make you younger and more vital. We hear our mother's voice, our father's voice, the voices in our community, on the radio, in the paper, on our box of Wheaties . . . and we respond. But the world of things is not reliable. The idea that it can provide lasting happiness is a little unspoken lie we all agree on, although experience tells us otherwise.

In his text *The Way of the Bodhisattva*, the renowned Indian scholar Shantideva talks about our tendency to search for happiness outside of ourselves. He says that if things had any inherent qualities, then those qualities should always be evident—they wouldn't ever change. For instance, if a pillow possessed inherent qualities of comfort, it would bring comfort even to a mother who has just lost her only child. All she would have to do is lie her head upon it and everything would be okay.

But in fact, there is no one thing that can make us happy. When we expect stability from the world of things we make ourselves vulnerable to disappointment. When things change, as they inevitably do, we think the phenomenal world has turned on us: people disappoint us, our bodies disappoint us, the pleasant feeling we got from our meditation session yesterday won't come back. Even chocolate cake and apple pie let us down. These pleasurable things now become the source of our unhappiness. "They're not working. Where did all the pleasure go?"

The fact that we can't ultimately depend on the world is not a punishment; it's just how things are. But where does it leave us? How do we appreciate life—our relationships, our physical bodies, Beethoven's Concerto no. 5 in E-Flat Major—without holding on to it as something that will last and continue to bring us pleasure? How can we find true inner happiness knowing that we are subject to uncertainty, old age, sickness, and death? The Buddha had not yet answered these questions when he cast away the rights to his kingdom.

REJECTING EXPERIENCE

If you've ever been to India you've seen the *sadhus*, or renunciants. Presently in India, a land of over one billion people, there are over thirteen million renunciants. Some wear their hair in long, matted locks, often twisted in a bundle on the top of their heads. They cover their almost-naked bodies with ash and they ritually smoke hashish, an austerity associated with non-attachment to the physical form. Many of them engage in extreme self-mortification practices, such as holding their arms up for the whole of their lives. Some wander in solitude. Others live in temples, caves, or at the foot of trees. Some gather in groups, while others sit silently alone in meditation. They can be lively, eccentric, and sometimes fierce. They bring a lot of color to the already colorful culture of India. India would not be India without them. One can imagine that things have not changed much since the time of the Buddha.

The Prince entered the next phase of his search during a time of affluence and thriving spirituality in India. Young Indian men who in harder times would have inherited their father's caste occupation began asking questions about the meaning of life and existence. They followed a growing trend of renunciants into a life of forest retreat, a tradition usually reserved for householders at the age of retirement.

The Prince studied with the accomplished teachers of his time. His practices included long periods of intense physical deprivation. For six years he sat diligently eating only the occasional seeds and herbs that blew into his lap. But six years of physical austerities left him weak and depleted to the point where his mind could barely function. The Prince concluded that this kind of aggression toward the body hindered spiritual development. He reached an understanding that, although he had cultivated an unwavering ability to still his mind, none of these practices addressed the nature of suffering and the path to true inner freedom he so desperately sought.

The Prince's guides taught that attaining the divine meant denying the physical. They viewed the physical world as base, lacking in meaning, and essentially a hindrance to liberation. However, the Prince's years in the forest revealed to him the value of the body as a support for the practice. He saw negating the rich expression of the physical world as a form of nihilism. He came to understand that spiritual development was not possible through suppressing what is clearly an undeniable part of the human experience.

During his time in the forest, the Prince engaged in a tradition that emerged from his disenchantment with the world of "things." Not finding happiness in the world of things, we naturally look for happiness aside from the world of things. The denial of the world of things shows up on the spiritual path when we think we can find an enlightenment that is divorced from our experience. As my friend once said, in jest, "I can't wait to attain enlightenment so I don't have to deal with all this bullshit." Let's face it, we all have this tendency to want to rocket off to another dimension . . . to be anywhere but here. We change the channel when the news gets too painful, because we don't know what to do with all this suffering. This process of selection edits out the uncomfortable pieces of our experience so that whatever we don't understand won't touch us: things feel just fine in our bubble. But can we really exclude the aspects of life that are so fundamental to the human experience? Suffering and uncertainty challenge our fantasy of a straight trip to nirvana. Denial is simply another extreme tendency that comes with false assumptions about the world. It is just the other side of trying to find happiness and security in the world of things.

After years of searching, the Prince reached a powerful conclusion: the world is precarious and uncertain and so there is no future in relying upon it for liberation. Yet he knew firsthand the impossibility of trying to attain liberation through denying what was simply right in front of him. "Chasing after or rejecting things only leads to despair," he thought. "How can I find the wisdom that transcends the limitations of these two approaches?" The Prince had not yet answered this question when he left his forest hermitage. But this very question escorted him to enlightenment.

2

The Middle Way

That the Buddha's question led to his awakening is a significant part of his story, and we should take note of it. In his story we will find a simple message: we access our greatest intelligence through engaging our life with the spirit of wonderment, not through seeking absolute conclusions.

If we think about it, life resists definition. How can we truly know things that continuously change, are impossible to pin down, and are always open to interpretation? Can we, for instance, ever reach absolute conclusions about the redness of a flower, a moment of grief, or the meaning of the universe?

We're lucky that the Buddha didn't simply reach a conclusion or settle for an answer. The world is full of answers. If you ask a simple question, you can get a million of them, no problem. In fact, think of how many conclusions we reach each day: think about all of our likes and dislikes, our views about the world, who we think we are, and who we decide we want to be. But have we ever been able to reach a point of absolute certainty about anything?

When the Buddha gave up hope in his search for answers, he

found an alternative he didn't know he had—the mind of an open question. The Buddha discovered that when he asked a question, his mind was engaged yet open. The process of inquiry itself protected him from the extremes of either ignorance or false certainty, providing room for the expression of mind's creative intelligence. He found a way of being in the mind of an open question that was profoundly clear, engaged, and full of adventure, and he called it the Middle Way.

The term *Middle Way* is commonly misunderstood. We may interpret *middle* to mean "finding a balance." For example, in the way that we might pursue, say, material fulfillment on the weekdays and try to balance that with something "spiritual" on the weekends. Or we may think the Middle Way refers to something in between two other things—such as a gap in between two moments of experience—or something ungraspable that is divorced from the world we know. But this is not the meaning of the Middle Way.

The Middle Way experience takes us altogether beyond thinking in extremes—beyond our usual assumptions about the world. It does not suggest we reject suffering to seek a nirvana elsewhere. It does not advise us to leave our ordinary functional life and enter a "spiritual" one instead. It does not affirm the existence of things, and it does not deny our experience of them either. Instead, the path of the Middle Way leads us through a process of inquiry that questions the nature of existence, non-existence, self, other, happiness, suffering, spirituality, and the world of experience. If we follow this process of inquiry, it will take us to a place of certitude beyond conclusions. This is exactly what happened to the Buddha.

3

The Tug of Me: Exploring the Nature of Self and Other

Up to this point we've followed the Prince into an exploration of the nature of suffering. We've seen him search for answers in the world of things and find nothing of lasting value. He entered altered states of consciousness through meditation practices aimed at transcending physical reality. But none of these practices addressed the nature of suffering and the path to true inner freedom. The Prince exhausted all views, assumptions, and possibilities.

Free of even the notions of enlightenment, the Prince rested in the mind of an open question. He trusted that something extraordinary was about to happen. And while sitting under the Bodhi Tree, the whole world opened up for him. This is how the Prince attained enlightenment and became the Buddha—the Awakened One. We might say that the Buddha's awakening sprang from the wide-open mind of his very own question.

The Buddha realized that his search for an answer to the end of suffering assumed a self that sought after happiness, yet was haunted by extinction. He understood how we try to maintain the familiar presence of self, whatever that means to us in each moment. Sometimes we affirm "me" and sometimes we protect "me." We bring desirable things toward "me" and push unwanted things away from "me" so that the parameters of "me" keep expanding and contracting. All this pulling and pushing fans the flames of strong emotions, and we try even harder to drive home the point: "I exist." Meanwhile, we live with the terror of an unavoidable death. We evaluate, organize, and struggle with everything we encounter in our attempts to substantiate the existence of a self. This is the relationship we have with our world.

Try to visualize your world without the tug of "me" with all its preferences: all its efforts to find stable ground in the world of things and protect itself from unwanted experiences. What would happen if, rather than organizing the world to suit the self, we stopped manipulating everything and instead just stayed present for our life?

Staying present challenges our habitual reactive tendencies. You may recognize this scenario: You're sitting at the dinner table, or in a room full of people, when suddenly everything falls quiet. The space feels pregnant, full of possibility, and then that one person— it may even be you—gets overwhelmed, uncomfortable, and just has to talk. This is how we deal with pregnant moments—we try to escape them through the continual re-creation of the self. We are not accustomed to bearing witness to our own experience— our life—without putting a lid on it, manipulating it, reaching a conclusion about it, or ascribing meaning to it in some way. But in doing this, do we ever have a full experience?

The Buddha wanted a full experience. He wanted to see what would happen if he stopped trying to escape the present through attempting to secure the self. Imagine him now sitting beneath the Bodhi Tree . . .

NO SELF IN THE BODY

The Buddha goes straight to the heart of the matter, which, of course, is the self. The Buddha looks for the self. Where does it reside? Does it have parameters? We usually define the self as being whatever everything else is not. But where do we actually draw that line? Where do we stop and where does our universe begin? Here we find the Buddha just warming up . . .

The Buddha looks at his physical body. The self seems to reside within the boundaries of the physical form. Yet he observes the inhalation and exhalation of his own breath—an exchange of his inner and outer worlds. His awareness turns to the food that sustains him; again two worlds come together. He feels the outer elements of space, air, fire, water, and earth weave through the fabric of his physical being. He witnesses the continuation of his ancestral line and all the constituents that brought his physical form into existence. He concludes that the body does not exist in isolation; it arises in dependence upon other.

The Buddha feels the weight of his body supported by the earth beneath him. We tend to think that if something is solid and substantial, it must exist as separate from other things. We might think, "I can touch my body. It feels like a thing. How can you say no boundaries exist between my body and everything else? It has a shape and feels real and solid to the touch." But the Buddha understands that the density, tangibility, or shape of an object doesn't give it more of an independent "thingness" than a soft or malleable object has, and neither do the sensations we feel through contact with objects make them more real. For instance, we may prick ourselves with a pin, but does the sharp sensation we feel verify the body's thingness? In fact, we can only feel the sharpness of the pin in dependence upon the pin itself. That we can feel the object doesn't prove its independent existence. In fact, it proves the opposite—that no thing exists separate from other elements. All things are equal in their dependence upon other, regardless of their qualities.

The Buddha observes that the body has no definitive form. If we were to take apart a human body and spread all its parts out on the floor, we could ask: where does this singular entity called "body" reside? How can we separate the body from its parts?

Everything is a composite of parts, the Buddha observes. And we define these parts by their parameters—their separateness from other parts. As long as a part has edges, as all things do, it has smaller parts. And, with our reasoning mind, we find within the edges of even the smallest of parts more parts and smaller parts, until we can't find the boundary of parts at all. And who could point to an edgeless part? In this way the Buddha discovers that even parts have no true parameters. He arrives at the realization of no-thingness.

The Buddha concludes that although the body appears and functions as the physical aspect of self, it has no limits—no boundaries. It is not something that exists in and of itself as separate from other. The Buddha understands that the body is infinite . . . yet he experiences the warmth, breath, and movement of his physical form.

No Self in the Mind

The Buddha is no longer warm; he is hot, hot, hot.*

He can't find the edges of his physical being. He concludes that if the self cannot be found within or outside the body then the self must reside in the mind. The Buddha looks for the edges of mind. Where does the mind leave off and our universe begin?

The Buddha's inquiry here is simple and direct, but we have to think about it. Do we ever question the nature of knowing? Do we ever consciously think about whether things exist or not? We assume a self. We feel the presence—the tug—of the self at all times. But we don't usually question where or what the self might be.

The Buddha's process of investigation can be challenging. This is not because his teachings are abstract but rather because they urge

---

*This common American expression indicates that someone is getting very close to finding what they're looking for. The phrase originates from a children's game, in which one child looks for a hidden object. The other children, in order to help direct the child toward what they're searching for, tell them whether they are getting hot, warm, or cold—in other words, close, medium, or far—in relation to their goal.

us to deeply explore our own experience. This direct exploration of experience marks the contribution of the Buddha's wisdom. It takes some mental muscle, but it serves an important purpose: it takes us to the heart of the matter.

So, the Buddha looks deeply into the nature of knowing and realizes that in the same way the body arises in dependence upon other elements, so too does our ability to know anything. Mind functions as the mirror upon which all forms, thoughts, emotions, and sensations reflect. When we look at our reflection in the mirror we cannot separate the mirror from our reflection in it. Mirrors, by definition, always reflect images—the image and the mirror depend upon each other. We cannot say that our reflection and the mirror are one and the same, nor can we say they are separate. Neither the same nor separate . . . we see the reflection of our face, clear and recognizable.

The Buddha feels the coolness of the moon on his skin. He understands that without the presence of the moon, he would not know its coolness or experience its luminous rays brightening the forested landscape. Mind, by definition, knows objects: our awareness and the moon depend upon each other. In knowing, our inner and outer worlds come together. The moon and our awareness are not the same, yet we cannot separate the moon from our awareness of it. Neither the same nor separate . . . we experience this luminous globe lighting up the world around us.

In our experience, all causes and conditions, our inner and outer worlds, the elements, all come together. But where is this thing called mind or self? Where is this central organizing principle?

The egg has burst . . . The Buddha awakens to a way of being with no center or edge. He finds no independent self or other, no inner or outer worlds, no center or periphery, no coming together or separation, no individuated mind or matter. Although the body and mind appear and we experience them, they are limitless, without boundary. If this is so, where could the self reside? Where do we begin and the world end? If self were to exist, the Buddha concludes, it would be as big as our universe, which is infinite.

4

The Buddha and
the Hot-Dog Vendor

When we don't yet have a direct experience of interdependence and boundarylessness things can get a little abstract and vague. For instance, sometimes when first encountering the Middle Way people think, "Well if we can't find the parameters of self and other it must mean that everything is one." Have you heard the joke: "What did the Buddha say to the hot-dog vendor?" "Make me one with everything." But what does that mean exactly? Does it mean that everything is the same? Most of us would argue that we don't experience the world in that way.

The Buddha didn't say that everything is one. He said that everything arises in dependence upon something "other." I think when people say that everything is one, they mean that they feel connected to everything around them—now, this *does* relate to the experience of interdependence. When we pay attention to language, we begin to understand important subtleties that change the way we see things.

Not the Same or Different

Another way of explaining the Buddha's statement that everything arises in dependence upon something other is to say things are "not the same nor are they different." For instance, self and the world we perceive are not the same, yet we cannot separate the world from our awareness of it. This is a powerful statement because it challenges our belief that things exist separately with their own parameters. But then, if self and what we perceive are not the same or different, where does that leave us? It actually doesn't *leave* us anywhere. It takes us beyond the limits of ordinary thinking—to the Middle Way. But in order to understand how this is so, we need to examine our views.

Just suppose we were the same or one with everything, how then would we function in ordinary life? How many tickets would we have to buy when we went to the movies? Whose teeth would we brush in the morning? What would our name be? If we were one with everything, could we use this argument to our advantage and try to get others to pay our bills? I doubt it. Nobody would go for it. It turns out that "everything being one" is something vague we sometimes say without reflecting upon what it really means.

At the same time we cannot say that we are separate from other. If we were truly independent, we would have no relationship to what we call "our world." If we were separate, we couldn't interact with anything. Forget about buying a movie ticket or brushing our teeth. Forget about knowing or touching or seeing anything other. Forget about experience in general. Fortunately, we can see through our own direct perceptions that this is not the case. Our interaction with the world defines our awareness in each moment. It is a lively and unpredictable exchange.

Not the same and not different leaves us with an understanding of relationship. It means that in relation to our son we are a mother; in relation to our mother we are a daughter; in relation to our teacher we are a student; in relation to the universe we are so, so small; in relation to a bug we are big and looming . . . and yet all these descriptions still don't lead us to conclusions about who we really are. This remains an open question. We are unfindable, elusive and unfinished, ever-fluctuating and dynamic, and we change with our world. Yet we still have to pay our bills, and we can be sure there is someone out there waiting to receive our payments.

That self and other are not the same or different gives us something to ponder. There is something freeing about all of this. There is something compassionate about this, too. This is the Middle Way. How amazing.

5

Two Means of Escape

Hundreds of years after the Buddha's enlightenment, a great scholar and illustrious follower of the Buddha, Nagarjuna, discovered the Middle Way teachings. And out of his love for them he exclaimed: "I pay homage to he who has abandoned all views."

Nagarjuna was speaking about the Buddha, of course. And the views he refers to cut far deeper than philosophy. For these are the subtle assumptions and beliefs we have about the world: namely, that happiness can be found within the world of things, or conversely, that we must reject the world to find happiness. These assumptions affect the very way we respond to things viscerally, energetically, emotionally, and conceptually.

The Buddha didn't just intellectually question these assumptions; he tried them on for size to see if they would fit. And when he found that they only led to wanting and rejection, excitement and anxiety, he gave up on them and sat in meditation beneath the Bodhi Tree. This is exactly what we have to do.

Meditation practice provides the perfect context for observing our beliefs and recognizing the tug-of-war we have with our own experience. Just sit quietly for five minutes and watch what happens. Unless we have some accomplishment in meditation, we won't know what to do with all the activity. We become overwhelmed by the energetic play of the mind, pummeled by our own thoughts and emotions, bewildered by our inability to sit in peace. We will want to do something. And we really only have two means of escape from all this mayhem: we can either spin out into thought, which is an exaggeration of experience, or we can suppress or deny it.

Exaggeration and denial describe the dilemma we have with mind, and not just in meditation. Exaggeration and denial operate in conjunction with all our fantasies, hopes, and fears. When we exaggerate experience, we see what isn't there. And when we deny it, we don't see what is. Both exaggeration and denial are extraneous to the true nature of things, the nature we experience when we just stay present.

EXAGGERATION

When we sit down to practice, it takes but a moment to spin out into thought—to get lost in fantasy. Suddenly we can't remember the date of our last tetanus shot. We start to go over our schedule. When can we see the nurse? But in the meantime, what if we step on a nail? What if we get lockjaw?

We take these thoughts so seriously. We get all worked up, feeling that it's all so important, and then, suddenly, someone coughs and the sound penetrates our fantasy bubble and it pops . . . Where are we?

Oh, right. We're on a group retreat in a room full of people. Our eyes were open but we didn't see a thing. Our ears were open but we didn't hear or feel the world around us because we basically had checked out. The practice instructions didn't enter our minds, because all the while we were tending to important imaginary matters, driven on by the momentum of our thoughts.

Exaggerations embed themselves in our individual thoughts and emotions as well as our national ones. We have seen how the stability or instability of our national economy, for instance, depends largely upon our individual and collective hopes and fears. Hopes and fears morph into speculations, fantasies, dreams, and nightmares—all of which show up on the path to the "American dream." While they may shape our economy, they certainly don't lead us into a direct relationship with reality.

Exaggeration disengages us from the present to one degree or another, which means we lose our connection to the world around us. In the case of the economy, when the prosperity bubble pops, it forces us back to life's basics: food and rent. We start to ask some basic questions: "How can I simplify my life? How can I adapt to the changes I see around me? Maybe I should start a garden, maybe get some chickens to farm some eggs."

In the case of meditation practice, when our fantasy bubble pops, we return to the basics of our breath, our bodies, our connection to other beings and the world around us, the wisdom of our tradition. All these things bring us back to the present moment. When we start to practice meditation, we may be astounded by how often our mind is off musing and how rarely we are awake to the basic realities of life. But soon the practice quiets our mind, and we begin to understand the difference between staying present and spinning out into fantasy. Meditation practice provides us with a context to question whether or not we even have a choice between relaxing with the rich energy of our experience or distracting ourselves with busy-ness.

Denial

After exaggeration, there is really only one other means of escape from the raw energy of experience: denial. And when we sit down to practice, there is always plenty of denial, suppression, and blocking.

Thoughts come with energy, sensation, and emotion, and that's no problem. But what do we do when the energy, sensations, thoughts, and emotions get uncomfortable? What do we do with all the unwanted experiences we have in meditation? The tension in our neck: what will we do with that? What about all those wild uncontrollable thoughts? What about dullness, negative emotions, fatigue, speed, nuttiness, boredom, and basic unpleasantness?

"Unwanted" refers to the disappointments we experience when our hopes and expectations of how we want things to be don't work out. We have preferences as to how our experience should be: a respite from ordinary life; some time out to be "spiritual"; a pleasant state of mind. But when we sit down to meditate, our mind just seems to rough us up. We don't know how to relate to the dynamic energy of mind, because it seems to come at us like an enemy. But the fact that we reject so much of our experience should indicate to us that we're on the wrong track.

Denial turns our awareness away from our discomfort in search of liberation despite our experience. Does this sound familiar? The Buddha left his forest hermitage because he realized that spiritual development was not possible through denial of the physical world, thoughts, emotions, and perceptions. In other words, he understood that attaining enlightenment was not possible through rejecting or denying the occurrences that make up our life.

The unique beauty and kindness of the Buddha's approach is that it never suggests we need to experience anything other than what we experience. The Buddha never said that some thoughts are bad or wrong and we should reject them. Thoughts and emotions—all manner of occurrences—arise in our lives, and we can't control them. Buddha's first teaching begins with a deep exploration of suffering and its causes. Buddhist contemplation provides us with an opportunity to develop a new relationship to suffering as opposed to our usual approach of denying unwanted experience. In this way, challenging circumstances become gateways for liberation. In this spirit, the Buddhist teachings emphasize the practice of including and deeply penetrating to the nature of all things rather than rejecting experiences.

Once, during a difficult retreat where a lot of turbulent thoughts and emotions kept arising in my practice, my teacher, Dzigar Kongtrül Rinpoche, explained to me that the disturbances I encountered came from a subtle resistance I had toward my experience. Rinpoche reminded me that the attitude of practice was to extend respect and gratitude toward mind and experience. When we respond to anything that arises with judgment or aggression, we experience the pain of it. The next time I sat down to practice I stopped pushing at my experience. It amazed me to see what a difference it made. It was such a small adjustment, yet I felt as if a heavy weight had been lifted. And most importantly, these instructions initiated me into enjoying my mind in practice.

CREATIVE ENERGY

Exaggeration and denial are the strategies reactive mind uses to avoid the natural creative energy that presents itself to us in each moment of experience. We can learn a lot by observing, in our own bodies, how we work with this energy. For example, say we have a strong rush of aggression, desire, or fear. A mix of thoughts, emotions, and physical sensations surges throughout our body. What do we do with that energy? People often say, "Go ahead, release it. Let it out. If you hold it in, it will just get worse." In one way this is true. This can happen. Yet when we continue to vent our anger, get excited and lose ourselves in the heat of the moment, or start to panic when we're afraid, we deplete our energy, lose our vibrancy, our composure and confidence. We often do things we wish we hadn't. We may suspect that perhaps we could have done things differently: rerouted our energy in a more positive direction . . . although we're not sure how. On the other hand, if we suppress this energy, it gets blocked and we get a tight neck, clenched jaw, stiff back, and shallow breath. We can watch our bodies harden and bend with age. Our way of working with energy shapes our physique, our posture, and the way we carry ourselves as we move through the world. It all has to do with how we respond to this incredible wealth of energy that can potentially flow through us in a natural and ordinary way.

The renowned twentieth-century meditation master Dilgo Khyentse Rinpoche had the most unusual physical presence I have ever seen. His body was grand and stable like a mountain, yet a soft, yielding, and vibrant energy seemed to flow through him unobstructed, like a river. I remember feeling struck by the unceasing quality of his teaching—there was no break in his speech: as he inhaled he taught and as he exhaled he taught. An unending stream of people came to see him each day, yet his compassionate energy and longing to serve others never diminished. How does someone with so many people under his care generate such deep reservoirs of energy?

One can only assume this was the result of his practice accomplishment: his ability to stay present and engaged without depleting the creative energy that ran through him by spinning off into excitement or anxiety. The qualities I observed in Dilgo Khyentse Rinpoche were something ordinary people, such as myself, could see. You can ask anyone who ever met him, and I'm sure they will tell you the same. I imagine the Buddha had a similar physical presence as he rested his mind in the wisdom of the Middle Way, beyond exaggeration and denial, beneath the Bodhi Tree.

The Fork in the Road

The purpose of practice is to habituate ourselves to openness. This means we need to understand reactive mind. How do we experience the difference between reacting and staying open?

At what point do we decide to go with the habitual tendencies of exaggeration and denial or try something new? Where is the fork in the road? We need to explore these two experiences: reacting . . . staying open . . . reacting . . . staying open . . . reacting . . . staying open again. We begin to see the difference. It's a process of refinement. Our investigation cultivates a discerning intelligence that guides us in a positive direction.

We need to ask ourselves: "If our confusion finds its genesis in our habit of turning away from the open state, what would happen if we habituated ourselves to staying open?" Surprise: another koan.

6

Knowing Things

When we speak about reactive tendencies of exaggeration and denial, we may wonder exactly what it is that we are reacting to. Think about this. How do you perceive things, and why do you respond to them in the way that you do?

We have different ways of knowing things. Most commonly we know "things" through our habitual objectification of them. For example, we often speak about the objectification of women. When we objectify something, we draw a boundary around it and therefore can only know it in a limited way. Who, for instance, is that sultry woman on the billboard—the one in that cool black dress holding a martini? Who is she aside from the one-dimensional image we have of her, an image based upon our fantasies, our desires or insecurities? Undoubtedly, she has a longing for happiness, like all of us. She also feels the pain that comes with that longing, which is touching and beautiful in its way.

Human beings are complex: we have fresh moments and rotten moments. We have creative and destructive moments, too. We are crazy and predictable, glorious and miserable. Sometimes human beings seem like the lowest form of life on earth . . . then suddenly we find someone doing something brilliant, touching, and humane. There is a depth and richness in a human being that we can never capture or pin down. In truth, everything is like this—like shifting sands. Try to find "things" if you can. Try to find them before you objectify them, hem them in with concepts, tamper with them, or embellish them by exaggerating or denying their existence. Do you see what I'm getting at here? No matter how hard we search, in the realms of science, psychology, or otherwise, we will never reach an absolute conclusion in the world of "things." The world that we objectify will never offer us a full experience. A full experience only comes from our ability to know the truth of thinglessness. When we speak about the boundarylessness of things, we are pointing to knowing their truth, or essence. As we saw before: we cannot find a true boundary or edge to any thing, because all things exist in dependence upon other things. When we experience the interdependent and boundaryless nature of things, we don't feel the heaviness of the world against us—the world as opposed to me. Instead we feel the fullness of the world, and we are part of that fullness. When we stop objectifying things, in effect, we have nothing other to react to.

TOLERATING THINGS

In Tibetan, the word *zopa* often translates as "patience," "endurance," or "tolerance." I don't think we have an English equivalent that describes the depth and meaning of this word—at least I haven't found one yet. While zopa has many usages, the most provocative I've found is described by the nineteenth-century wandering yogi Patrul Rinpoche, in his text *The Words of My Perfect Teacher*. He describes zopa as "the ability to bear the truth of thinglessness or boundarylessness." What does it mean to tolerate thinglessness? Good question.

Normally, "tolerating" something means "putting up with" it.

We tolerate things on principle. We tolerate things we cannot change and things we'd rather not confront for fear of the consequences. We tolerate the coffee at the office, our neighbor's dog, that nasty recurring rash on our cheek, and our own and others' idiosyncrasies.

Tolerating the boundarylessness of things—zopa—is different. It means that we change our attitude toward the thing itself, whatever that thing may be: a challenging state of mind, the redness of the sunset reflecting on a beautiful mountain, pleasant and unpleasant meditation experiences, our boss. We experience a shift of habit when we stop objectifying, embellishing, or turning away from the fullness of expression. We start to know things in a different way. To bear or tolerate thinglessness means not running away from a bigger experience.

The way we know things depends upon the mind, nothing more. Most of us have moments of deep contentment when we don't feel a need to alter, express, run from, or invest some special meaning in our experience in any way. Deep contentment shows us that, at least momentarily, our habit of cherishing and protecting ourselves from what we call "other" has subsided. In moments like these, we have stopped objectifying things. We can let things be. And when the mind rests at ease in this way, it accommodates everything, like space.

Space, by nature, allows objects to come into being, to function, to expand, to contract, to move around, and to disappear without interference. Space doesn't do—it allows. It never creates objects, and it never destroys them, which is just another way of saying that space doesn't elaborate upon or reject what moves through it. Space relies upon nothing, yet everything relies upon the yielding nature of space. For this reason, the most prolific writer and meditation master of the Nyingma lineage, Kunchyen Longchenpa,* talked

---

*Kunchyen Longchenpa (fourteenth century) was the most famous and important scholar-meditation master of the Nyingma school of Tibetan Buddhism. He was responsible for compiling, expounding upon, and writing commentaries on the vast literature of the Great Perfection, thus preserving these teachings, which have become widespread.

about space as the universal metaphor for the mind that finds the Middle Way of being.

THE TRUTH OF THINGS

Initially, as we search for the Middle Way, we will need a little boost—a bit of strength and verve to be exact—in order to be able to abide in thinglessness. What will happen? We don't know. And we haven't yet habituated ourselves to the spacious quality of mind. Our longstanding impulse to objectify and run with our experiences is virtually automatic. So we should know, "going in," that a little discomfort may arise. That's what happens when we break any habit, isn't it?

Although tolerating thinglessness seems foreign to us, we actually do it all the time. Think of what happens when we ask a question: curiosity and wonder keep our mind in suspense, and we engage our experience without objectifying it. Our mind stays wide open, alert, and ready for possibility. We may even say we have reached the height of our intelligence when we ask a question.

Koans take the art of questioning into the realm of practice. Koans are questions that emerge from dualistic, conceptual mind. Yet we cannot answer them in the same way in which we asked them. In search of an answer they take us beyond the mind of objectification. We usually associate koans with Zen practice. Perhaps Zen practitioners got the idea of koan practice from the Buddha himself.

My friend Larry studied koans with his Zen teacher, the late Kyudo Nakagawa Roshi, for many years. He once told me that Roshi would often give different students the same koan to study. Sometimes the students would come to Roshi with similar answers. Roshi might dismiss the answer from one student and accept the same answer from another student. The reason for this, as Larry explained it to me, had to do with whether or not the student presented the answer with the confidence of a direct experience. In other words, the purpose of a koan is to transcend the dualism of the question in order to arrive at the Middle Way of being. When the student had arrived in this way, Roshi was satisfied. Otherwise, no matter how clever or correct the answer was, to Roshi it was just another answer.

We may recall that the Buddha grappled with a koan: "How can beings find happiness in the face of old age, sickness, and death?" The Buddha's question assumed an objectified self that yearned for freedom from an objectified notion of suffering. By definition his question was dualistic. Yet his answer, as you may remember, emerged from the realization of boundarylessness. It took him beyond the realm of objectified things and objectified self. It revealed to him a whole new way of knowing things—a way of knowing free from the struggle and limits of ordinary dualistic mind.

We can never reach a conclusion about the Middle Way through objectification. Boundarylessness, by definition, is inconclusive. What we can know, however, is the profound fullness and limitless nature of all things. To know things in this way is the experience of liberation.

7

No Words for Liberation

When the Buddha attained enlightenment beneath the Bodhi Tree, he couldn't put words to the profundity of his experience. He resolved to keep his discovery to himself, assuming no one would understand. This, of course, didn't last long. Inspired by his presence, many came to see him to request teachings. Touched by the pain of the human condition, he taught them with great clarity and tenderness.

However, the Buddha's initial concern raises an important question: how do we describe an experience beyond words? How can we speak about something that cannot be objectified? The moment we try to wrap our conceptual mind around an experience, we lose it. We reduce the limitless quality of being to a thing.

Many scholars debate this point in the Middle Way tradition. Some schools lead us through a process of investigation that shows us what liberation is not. In other words, when the proponents of these schools exhaust all misconceptions regarding the nature of things, they let the conceptual mind rest. They don't try to describe something that can never be objectified. Other schools disagree

with this approach. They put words to the experience of boundarylessness, words such as *compassion, wisdom, skillful actions,* and *love.*
They assert that these qualities arise as a direct result of realizing
boundarylessness. They believe that if these qualities remain un-
articulated, those who study the Middle Way may misinterpret
thinglessness as the absence of experience—like a void.

Buddhist practitioners and scholars also draw on traditional
metaphors to describe the experience of awakening, such as
Longchenpa's use of space as the universal metaphor for the boundaryless nature of mind. Metaphors are suggestions that can spark
understanding through personal experiences. In the Vajrayana tradition, mature students receive transmission through metaphor
or pointing-out instructions from a qualified teacher, who in this
way introduces them to the boundaryless nature of mind.

But in the end, liberation is inexpressible. As it says in the
Dzogpa Chenpo, or Great Perfection literature,* trying to describe
such an experience is like a mute person trying to describe the
taste of sugar.

SMALL AWAKENINGS

Although we can't describe awakened mind, it certainly doesn't
mean we can't wake up. If you think about it, we live and move
about in the state of boundarylessness at all times, so just by default
we're bound to experience the truth of things here and there. And
we need to recognize these blessings when they arise. A moment of
unbiased loving care toward another being, for instance, frees us
from the bondage of our own self-centeredness. Dzigar Kongtrül
Rinpoche always says that the power of these small gestures, those
we tend to underestimate, can sustain us for an entire day.

---

*The Dzogpa Chenpo (rDzogs-Pa Ch'en-Po) teachings are the most essential and developed
teachings of the Nyingma, or Old Translation School, lineage. They are the direct instructions that lead to the natural primordial state of unconditioned mind.

There is a movie starring Hugh Grant in which the main character is a selfish, depressed, middle-aged bachelor living off his inheritance. Basically he has nothing to do all day but think about himself, which, needless to say, makes him miserable. Then, somewhere along the line, he rather unintentionally befriends a boy and later finds himself buying the unhappy adolescent a pair of tennis shoes. As he pays the cashier, he has an epiphany: he feels the warmth and goodness of his own generosity. He realizes that giving to others makes him happy. And it startles him. It's such an innocent moment and yet so comically tragic, because we realize that this thirty-eight-year-old man has just figured this out.

This may seem like a trite example, but these little openings—these small awakenings—reveal to us the best of who we are and what we can know. A moment of compassion, a moment of resting in the present rather than trying to escape it, a moment of appreciation for anything other than what is good for me, a moment of rejoicing in the good qualities of others, a moment of resting in the boundaryless nature of things, even a moment of aspiring to cultivate altruistic qualities—all of these emancipate us from the bondage of our own ignorance.

As meditation practitioners, we need to recognize and engage the magical aspects of experience that move us away from a contracted sense of self and other and toward the truth of things—toward these small awakenings. Because, when you think about it, isn't that the point of practice: liberation?

8

The "E" Word

We have to make up a lot of words to express the ineffable experience of the Middle Way: *boundarylessness*, *thinglessness*, *unfindableness*, a lot of -*ness* words. But these words all point to a more traditional term, one that seems even more challenging for most people: *emptiness*, also known as the "E" word among Buddhists.

The "E" word often scares people. Everything is empty? What does that mean? We think something vital—our life force—will be taken away if we agree that things are empty. We think of the glass half empty, empty words, empty wallet, empty nest, an empty feeling in my chest—a vacuum, deprivation, loneliness, hollowness, doom, gloom, nothingness.

But imagine yourself in New York City during rush hour in desperate need of a cab. When you can hail an empty one, it only means possibility for you. We can't write a book without an empty piece of paper, and when our schedule is empty we can do anything we want. Hooray for emptiness. Emptiness signifies possibility. Emptiness allows for more room—in fact, limitless room—for things to arise. But it doesn't just make room for things; it describes their very nature. So when we realize the nature of emptiness, it means we know the boundaryless nature of things. Emptiness is just another way of saying that we can know things without objectifying them. Paradoxically, we can't even talk about having a full experience without emptiness. Think about that.

I want to pay tribute to the word *emptiness*. It's one of the most profound words in Buddhist literature, and it lies at the very heart of the Buddha's teachings. The sutras often refer to emptiness as the Mother Prajnaparamita—the Mother of Transcendent Wisdom. The "mother" refers to the natural womblike quality of emptiness that is pregnant with possibility.

In the Prajnaparamita literature,* it says that just as children of a mother who has fallen ill wholeheartedly preoccupy themselves with her wellness, the bodhisattvas who seek liberation through the practice of the Middle Way wholeheartedly preoccupy themselves with Mother Emptiness. Their attentiveness to her leads to fully knowing her. In knowing her, they find liberation—Buddhahood. The imagery and warmth expressed in this traditional language reveal that emptiness is central to awakening.

Writing a book about the Buddha's Middle Way without using the "E" word is challenging. But *emptiness* is a packed word, which means it takes a lot of study and contemplation to break it open and understand it in the context of meditation practice. By choosing not to use the "E" word in this book, I was forced to explore the meaning of emptiness more deeply. But I mention it here because emptiness holds a central place in the context of Buddhist scholarship and literature. I wouldn't dismiss the "E" word too quickly if I were you. It's a great word, but we probably won't see it again in this book.

---

*This is a paraphrase from Edward Conze's translation of the *Ratnagunasamcaya-gatha*, titled *The Perfection of Wisdom in Eight Thousand Lines and Its Verse Summary*, p. 31, verse 253.

9

As Big as Our World

Many years ago, when we first moved to Colorado, Dzigar Kong-trül Rinpoche and I were driving on a winding mountain pass in the Rockies. It was September, and the aspens were turning. You don't see a lot of yellow, orange, and red in the arid climate of the Rockies—except in the autumn. In the autumn, the sunlight hits the leaves and they shimmer. I felt so overwhelmed by this beauty, I was almost agitated by it. I kept saying, "How beautiful it is, how beautiful, how beautiful . . ." Rinpoche turned to me and asked: "Is it *too* beautiful for you?" This got me thinking . . . even beauty can cause us pain when we objectify it.

The shape of our life has less to do with what we encounter than with our relationship to it. When we objectify experience—be it beauty or pain—we enter into a relationship of struggle with our world—a world all about "me."

But life is not something that happens *to* us. We can't separate ourselves from the constant stream of experience we call our life. We are not victims of our life, and we are not unworthy of our life either. Life is not too beautiful or divine for us. It is not too big or painful or frightening or even too complicated for us, although at times it may seem that way. Our challenge, as human beings, is to make ourselves big enough to accommodate all of it.

EMBRACING OUR HUMANNESS

"Accommodating all of it" as a practice means embracing our humanness in all its glory and confusion. It means accepting the beauty, ugliness, joy, and pain of the world—our world—and all its mystery, ambiguity, and contradiction, too. How do we live a life we can't hold on to? How do we enjoy a piece of chocolate cake when a child in Africa has cholera? How do we reconcile "me" with "enlightenment"? Who can answer these kinds of questions? No one can. But we can embrace their mystery.

Accommodating all of it is a heart practice, because we are inviting life rather than rejecting it. This practice expresses the fundamental principle of nonviolence, because we can't hold others responsible for our happiness and pain. We can't point a finger at the government and say, "That's why my life sucks." We can't objectify things in this way when we practice. But we can take on our life knowing that each moment of it arises in connection to a grand and unfathomable landscape, of which we are an integral part. We are naturally big—naturally infinite—like everything else.

As we begin the practice of accommodating all of it, we may feel intimidated by the wild and unruly character of our thoughts and emotions. But as we learn to habituate ourselves to openness rather than objectifying things, we come to know the nature of thoughts and emotions. We can't truly find these things we usually shrink away from or react to. They move and change and arise in dependence upon other things.

Knowing this loosens up the whole atmosphere of the mind. We may recall that when we first started practicing meditation, we could only relax with about 20 percent of our experience, but as we practiced we could relax with 30 percent . . . then 40 percent . . . or more. As we practice we may even develop a passion to understand experiences that have always frightened us—experiences we've tried to avoid. Practice engenders this kind of boldness.

The practice of accommodating all of it includes all the things we like and don't like; this allows us the freedom to be a full human being without the agitation that comes from trying to sort, manage, and label our experience. If we do this practice for a while, we start to see that even suffering is full of possibility.

Developing a New Relationship to Suffering

The investigation of suffering marks our entranceway onto the Buddhist path. In so many words the Buddha taught us to behold, or accommodate, suffering. Suffering has something to offer us.

Suffering is not a personal matter, according to the Buddha's teaching. Suffering points to the nature of the world of things and the inability of that world to satisfy or bring about lasting happiness. Ajahn Sumedho, of the Buddhist Thai forest tradition, wrote a beautiful book on Buddha's Four Noble Truths,* of which the first truth is the truth of suffering. He describes the sensory world as a sensitive experience where we are continuously exposed to pleasure, pain, and the dualism of the human condition. This is the way it is. This is the result of birth. He says that when we admit this truth into our consciousness, it is not from the perspective that "I am suffering" but, rather, "there is suffering."

In the life story of the Buddha there is a poignant anecdote that illustrates the shift of perspective from "I am suffering" to "there is suffering." One day a woman named Gotami approached the

---

*The first teaching the Buddha gave immediately after his enlightenment. The four truths are the truth of suffering, the truth of the causes of suffering, the truth of the cessation of suffering, and the truth of the path.

Buddha clutching the body of her dead infant in her arms. She begged the Buddha to bring the child back to life. The Buddha said that he could help her but that she must first do something for him: he asked her to bring him back a mustard seed from a house in her village in which no one had died. The woman followed the Buddha's instruction but returned empty-handed. There was no household in the village that hadn't seen death. But in the process of looking, something had changed in Gotami. Her failure to collect a single mustard seed had shown her the universality of suffering. It had evoked in her compassion for the plight of all living beings. Moreover, she experienced the bravery that comes from acceptance. Gotami was able to make the shift from "I am suffering" to "there is suffering." Only then could she put down the body of her son.

My friend Robin lost her son as he was just moving into young adulthood. She said that after his death she joined a support group with other parents who had also experienced the loss of a child. Witnessing their grief she was able to move from "I am suffering" to "there is suffering." She wears a mustard seed in a locket around her neck to remind her of Gotami and her search.

BEHOLDING SUFFERING

When we turn our minds toward an honest reflection on the nature of suffering, what happens? We encounter a fuller experience of our life. The Buddha knew this and that is why he turned his mind directly toward suffering—the very thing most of us spend our lives trying to avoid. Through doing this, the Buddha illustrated to us that to behold suffering—to admit suffering into our experience—reflects the spirit of bravery we need to awaken.

The Buddha called this reflection on suffering the First Noble Truth. We must know that the Buddha only called suffering a "truth" in order to acknowledge that living beings experience it. Suffering itself possesses no inherent reality. Essentially, like all "things," suffering arises and falls away due to its dependence upon causes and conditions. Therefore, it has no identifiable boundaries. It is just another experience that cannot be objectified, captured, or pinned down. What is suffering before we objectify it? That's a good question.

10

Fixing and Healing

Our usual modus operandi is to try to rid our lives of suffering through rearranging things. Rather than admitting suffering into our experience, we tend to manufacture hopeful strategies of avoidance. My friend Buddy, a structural integration practitioner, says that a client will often walk into his office expecting to get "fixed"—to arrive at a physical state that is totally pain-free. This is not an unreasonable desire. Nobody wants to suffer. But we need to ask ourselves: "Is this mysterious, dynamic organism we inhabit fixable? Does it ever reach a final state of equanimity, where it no longer feels the movement, the pleasure and the pain, of the infinite universe it is a part of?"

Fixing differs from healing—it differs in attitude. Fixing aims at avoiding pain through trying to return to the good old days when we were pain-free. It has that kind of nostalgia; we just want to get back to the way things were. Such an attitude doesn't require us to change or to fully experience our bodies. We have a goal, but we are absent for the process that leads to that goal—a process that requires us to have a new experience, a new understanding of our physical form and how we inhabit it. The fixing approach doesn't get at the causes and conditions that gave rise to our ailment. It simply rearranges our physical confusion in a way that may offer us a little relief—usually temporary—from an undesirable sensation.

I don't know about you, but I often find myself waiting for a perfect state of physical equilibrium. "When is it going to happen? When will the day come that I feel consistently perfect?" But in truth, the body is not a fixable thing. As His Holiness the Dalai Lama said: "Physical happiness is just an occasional balance of elements in the body, not a deep harmony. Understand the temporary for what it is."* The body is, in fact, a dynamic and unpredictable organism, dependent upon parts, dependent upon elements, dependent upon everything else in the universe—a koan unto itself. Understanding this leads to healing. This understanding challenges us to participate in the unraveling of our own personal mystery rather than waiting for a final result. How can we accommodate the changes in our body to help it move in the direction of wellness? We may even relax with the physical sensation of pain a little . . . is it really as solid as we think? Maybe we don't have to go back to the way things were . . . maybe things can be different instead. What would that be like? We have to include our entire person—in fact our entire world—along with all the sensations we may not want, in order to heal.

The point is that healing doesn't promise us that things will work out the way we initially want them to. It doesn't promise us a cure for old age, sickness, and death. It doesn't promise a pain-free life. But it does promise a fundamental wellness—a wellness found within.

My mother, who spent many years working with people who had life-threatening illnesses, said she witnessed many of them

*His Holiness the Dalai Lama, *Mind of Clear Light: Advice on Living Well and Dying Consciously* (New York: Atria Books, 2003), p. 89.

move from states of physical and emotional "dis-ease" to a place of deep acceptance of their physical condition, their life, and their death. When people go through such experiences their whole demeanor changes; their outlook broadens. They no longer want to go back . . . they want to move forward. And as they move forward they have no regrets. She heard them say things like, "This disease was the greatest blessing of my life."

On National Public Radio I heard a woman talk about her experience with her daughter, a heroin addict who lived on the street. She tried taking her to rehab, talking to her, intervening in various ways, but to no avail. Finally, this courageous mother came to accept her daughter's situation. And rather than trying to rehabilitate or change her, she just went and sat with her in the park—she started to bear witness to the truth of her daughter's predicament. In one way, her story as she told it remained unresolved. She was unable to fix it. And yet, as a listener, I could feel the bravery and clarity that came from this woman's ability to work with her situation in a healing way.

True Strength

What did it take for that mother to sit by her daughter without trying to change her? The strength, or "tolerance," it takes to heal has nothing to do with a grin-and-bear-it machismo. True strength is like a flexible lacquer bowl—if you drop it, it will bounce—as opposed to a hard ceramic one that shatters into a hundred pieces. Strength is a soft, agile, and open mind that bears witness to life, rather than trying to fight against or live around undesirable experiences. Strength is our willingness to stay present in the face of uncertainty.

Because the Buddha urged us to behold suffering, people often misunderstand the Buddhist path as a path of suffering. I remember reading a magazine article whose author, in reference to Buddhism, wondered why anyone would want to participate in a religion that held the view "life is suffering." But this assumption reflected the author's own misunderstanding. What good is suffering? It can make us bitter. The transformative aspect of suffering comes about through the realization that we're big enough to face this inevitable aspect of life.

The great beings of all traditions understand the principles of accommodating all of it. They accept life and don't try to live around it. This means that they bear witness, along with everything else, to pain and sadness, which is why the wise—although free at heart and full of mirth—always have a glimmer of sadness in their eyes.

Developing a New Relationship to Beauty

I have one more tree story. One spring, years after driving down that winding road lined with autumn aspen trees, Rinpoche took me to Kyoto in Japan to see the cherry blossoms. The blossoms looked like a reflection of pink sunset on snow. I could go on about their beauty . . . but something interested me even more than the blossoms: observing Japanese people appreciating them.

When the Japanese look at cherry blossoms, if they say anything at all, they say something like: "Sakura [that means "cherry blossoms"] . . . ahhh . . ." "Ahhh . . ." might not be the best phonetic interpretation of the sound they make, but it is similar in sound and equivalent in meaning to "ahhh," the sound of wonder in English. "Ahhh . . ." is not a sound of objectification. That's more like "hmmm" (a sigh of doubt) or "yep" (I already know) or "by George!" (I think I've got it). The sound of wonder is not cerebral. Particularly when the Japanese say it, it sounds a bit like a sigh—it has a little sadness in it. It is the recognition of ephemeral beauty: beauty and decay go together, and the Japanese seem to understand that. Life is bittersweet. But here I am already starting to reach conclusions about people and trees again. Could the "ahhh" just be the expression of sheer openness? I wonder.

"Ahhh" comes from relaxing the muscles in our slightly opened mouth and letting the breath out in a natural way. It's effortless. Why don't you try it? It can evoke a sense of deep relaxation. I'm not the first to notice—this is ancient knowledge. The sound *ah* is the Sanskrit seed syllable for boundarylessness or space. They say in Sanskrit that *ah* is inherent in all the consonants in the Sanskrit alphabet, such as the letters *ra*, *sa*, or *ka*. In other words, consonants can only arise or move in the space of *ah*.

What do Japanese cherry blossom appreciators experience when they say, "*Sakura*, ahhh . . ."? I don't know. But I suspect it has something to do with appreciating beauty without objectifying it—creating space in the mind for a full experience of things.

PURE POTENTIAL

Mind is pure potential—it has no limits as to what it can hold, which means, of course, that we as living beings have no limits as to what we can hold, be it wretched or sublime, cranky or joyous, ugly or beautiful.

But beware, because when we stop objectifying things and instead admit them into our awareness, we won't see them in the same way as we did before. The lines between suffering and happiness will start to shift and fade. We may see traces of pain, expectation, and discontent in what we used to consider only "pleasant." Conversely, we may start to value what we previously considered "unwanted" as broadening and enriching. And this may rouse our curiosity enough that we begin to ask ourselves: "What is suffering or beauty before we objectify it?" Now if we're going to seriously start asking questions like this we better get ready to change . . . because that's what will happen.

II

Embracing Complexity

After reading the previous chapter, my father challenged me by saying: "That all sounds well and good, but there are some pretty misguided hombres out there in the world motivated by greed and profit. Some children don't have enough to eat. How do you accommodate that kind of injustice?"

I pondered this for a while . . . it's a good question, because it brings social action and ethical conduct into the equation. At the same time, within his question lies a mistaken assumption that accepting the unfixable nature of the human condition is passive or uncaring and disengages us from the world. So I rephrased his question: "How do we respond to situations intelligently and with care, knowing we can't fix them?" There's a koan for you.

We can work in a soup kitchen, we can vote, we can recycle, we can adopt stray animals, sign petitions, bring our neighbor soup when he's sick, provide shelter to those in need, throw out an evil dictator, express love and care in every possible situation . . . and what could be more noble? But it still won't change the fact that the world of things is ultimately unfixable.

Mahatma Gandhi, the foremost proponent of nonviolent action the world has ever known, devoted his life to working toward Indian independence from the British Empire. His bravery and intelligence lit up the world. Yet look at India and Pakistan since Partition . . . still in conflict. This doesn't reflect shortcomings on the part of Mahatma Gandhi. It just illustrates that the world of things will never reach a state of peaceful equilibrium. It will never satisfy us. It will never quench our thirst, even for peace.

INCONCLUSIVENESS

Why can't the world reach a state of peaceful equilibrium? Why can't we fix things? Simply because we can't pin things down . . . they are too complex.

My friend Kelly says that when she listens to the news she hears so much conflicting information she can't truly reach a conclusion about anything—a common experience. Usually we see this as a problem. Our inability to reach conclusions makes us feel ignorant and helpless. We feel pressured to sort it all out.

But think about this: maybe experiencing complexity brings us closer to reality than does thinking we've actually figured things out. False certainty doesn't finalize anything. Things keep moving and changing. They are influenced by countless variables, twists and turns . . . never for a moment settling into thingness.

So maybe we should question the accuracy or limitations of this kind of false certainty. Conflicting information confuses us only when we're trying to reach a definite conclusion. But if we're not trying to reach a conclusion in the first place—if we just observe and pay attention—we may actually have a fuller, more accurate reading of whatever we encounter. Let me give you an example.

In the movie *Dead Man Walking*, Sean Penn plays a disturbed young man who, with his equally disturbed friend, rapes a young woman and then goes on to kill her and her boyfriend. The movie follows him to his death by lethal injection. Meanwhile, it also follows the families of the victims, some of whom support his death sentence and others who don't. This movie takes a subject—the difficult subject of capital punishment—and looks at it from all angles. It never divides. It never deifies or vilifies anyone—as most Hollywood productions do. It never once reaches a conclusion. It simply looks at and lets you feel each point of view. Because it withholds all judgment in this way, I found myself walking out of the movie theater with a deep faith in human nature.

The genius of this movie is that it allows the viewer to feel tenderness for every single one of the characters—including the guilty protagonist. This kind of approach engages our deepest intelligence. It shows us that we can know things without reifying them; that we don't have to take a side in order to access our discerning intelligence; that we can function from a wide-open mind; that, in fact, our intelligence and compassion increase with receptivity.

In the Middle Way tradition, a philosophical school called the Prasangika Madhyamika turns "not taking a side" into a practice. The proponents of this school never make conclusive statements or take doctrinal stances. Instead they question their opponents' views and draw out the faults and inconsistencies of their arguments. Because Prasangika scholars don't reach conclusions about things, no one can trump them in debate. Yet their process of questioning brings everyone involved to a place of great openness and clarity.

Fundamentalism

Unfortunately, when faced with the world's ambiguity, instead of asking questions, we tend to withdraw into our familiar habit of objectification. We assume we already know how things are, and we can bypass uncertainty and ambiguity altogether. But think of how this false sense of security just denies us a fuller more intelligent understanding of things.

Chris Hedges, a Pulitzer Prize–winning journalist who covered the war in Bosnia, told a magazine interviewer: "If you acknowledge the moral ambiguity of human existence and the frightening non-rational forces that drive human beings and societies, it causes anxiety or neurosis. There is always a temptation to retreat into . . . 'tribal groups.' . . . Retreating into tribal groups is a way to revert to a child-like state of security, rather than live as an adult and struggle with ambiguity."*

Sometimes, when we struggle with understanding the religious and ideological extremism we hear about in the news, we wonder, "How do people get that way? Why don't they listen to each other?" But if we really want to understand it, all we have to do is look at ourselves. We all struggle with ambiguity, and we all have tendencies toward fundamentalism. How often do we objectify people and situations by putting them into a box: "He is like this; she is like that"? We have fundamentalist attitudes toward others when we simply refuse to let them be bigger than our subjective, objectified view of them.

Embracing complexity liberates the mind from the disturbing emotions associated with judgment and fundamentalism. When we stop objectifying things, we can't help but feel a tenderness toward the world. The tenderness we feel when we stop objectifying others is, again, so brilliantly illustrated in Dead Man Walking. When we are introduced to the protagonist's mother and his family, we suddenly realize, "Oh, he is not only a murderer, he is a son and a brother too." We start to see his vulnerabilities, what influenced him, his own fears, and the pain in his inability to look at the wretchedness of his actions. Because we start seeing more of him, as viewers we hang in there and eventually witness his painful and inspiring awakening. And we realize that a refusal to see him as anything but evil would have only cut us off from our own wisdom and compassion.

I'm curious to see what my father says about my response to his question. Not surprisingly, it brought me back, yet again, to the

---

*Interview with Bethany Saltman, "Moral Combat: Chris Hedges on War, Faith, and Fundamentalism." The Sun, no. 396, December 2008.

Middle Way and my fascination with the power of an open question. But it also inspired me to clear up what I see as a common misconception: that we will lose our clarity and intelligence if we give up our strong views. We believe that embracing complexity will immobilize us. As I write this book and contemplate the wisdom of the Dharma, as I listen and talk to others, and as I observe the world around me, I become more and more convinced that embracing complexity unlocks the profundity, intelligence, and compassion of our humanness.

12

With All Our Might

Surely, if the human condition could be fixed, the Buddha would have fixed it long ago. I'm sure Mother Teresa or Mahatma Gandhi would have cracked the code. And certainly the Dalai Lama would see to it that something was done. The overwhelming kindness of history's great luminaries, both past and present, is that despite knowing the unfixable nature of things, they did everything they could to serve others. In fact, they tried with all their might.

Temple Grandin is an expert in animal behavior and has deep insight into animal mind. She attributes this understanding to having been born autistic. She has observed that some patterns of animal behavior resemble the mental, emotional, and physical patterns she and others with autism experience. She is well known for having designed stockyard and slaughterhouse facilities that reduce fear and stress in cattle. A radio interviewer* recently asked her, "Why bother creating more humane conditions for animals

---

*"Fresh Air," National Public Radio, January 5, 2009.

that are about to be slaughtered anyway?" Ms. Grandin replied, "Why else, but to reduce their suffering."

Whatever we can do to serve others, at any moment, in any situation, is the practice of bodhi, or awakening. Service awakens in us a natural generosity, not a calculated response that weighs the pros and cons and decides whether it's worth the effort. It is a matter of the heart. We see a need and naturally move toward it. Shantideva, in The Way of the Bodhisattva, says that if our hair were on fire we would be obsessed with putting it out. In the same way, the process of awakening through service is the obsession of a bodhisattva.

BIG ASPIRATIONS

Once I drove from my home in Crestone, Colorado, to pick up my brother in Santa Fe, New Mexico—about a three-and-a-half-hour drive. On my way I stopped at a gas station and saw that the lottery was up to one hundred and seventy million dollars, so I bought a ticket. On the drive I thought, "What could I do with one hundred and seventy million dollars?" Hmmm . . . I could financially support members of my spiritual community so they could practice meditation and afford to work solely in service of the Dharma . . . I could build a healing center and a hospice in my town . . . fix up the horse stables . . . support my teacher in an extended retreat . . . sponsor my friend who paints beautiful devotional paintings . . . Three and a half hours later I found myself in Santa Fe feeling unusually fresh and resolved. Without noticing, I had not dedicated a single moment of my fantasy to what I could get for myself. And this, I realized, explained why my mind felt so at ease. Rinpoche always says that focusing on the happiness of others is the purest form of happiness. What could be truer?

On the bodhisattva path we make big aspirations: "May I attain Buddhahood for the benefit of all beings"; "May I bring all beings to enlightenment"; "May I take the suffering of others onto myself so that they can experience a life free of suffering." Sometimes we say these things without believing them. I remember one student actually trying to prove, with a calculator, the impossibility that all beings could attain enlightenment.

"Can we, can't we?" That's not the point. The point is to try with all our might. And only when we try with all our might do we see how service affects us, and how it affects others . . . and then we understand.

Simple Gestures

Serving others doesn't have to be grand. Extending a warm gesture to someone that we don't even know—say, on the bus—can make a tremendous difference to that person. It can bring them out of a deep place of isolation. Together, we share a moment of humanity. It's priceless.

In his film *Land of Silence and Darkness*, Werner Herzog documents the work of Fini Straubinger, a deaf-blind woman dedicated to bringing others in the deaf-blind community out of their deeply withdrawn state of aloneness. She "speaks" to them through tactile translation—a system of communication that consists of tapping and stroking different areas on the palm of the hand. As we watch her work, we wonder, "What would it be like to have so little sensory input?" Without this kind of communication, deaf-blind people would be totally cut off from the world. As one person says to Fini, "When you let go of my hand you could be a thousand miles away."

In the film, we watch Fini first tenderly make contact with, and then hand over a radio to, twenty-two-year-old Vladimir, who is not only deaf and blind but also has Down syndrome. Vladimir can't walk, he can't communicate, he can't dress himself. When we're first introduced to him, we see him alone, making sounds and hitting himself with a ball. He tries to understand the body he inhabits. He tries to understand himself in relationship to other things, in the environment he lives in. When Fini hands him the radio, although he can't see or hear, he feels the vibration of the music, and he clenches it in his arms as if he were making it a part of him. We see him come out of his isolation for that moment and become a part of something bigger—this vibrating, pulsating, energetic thing in his arms. That single moment brings home to us the importance of human interaction and love. And, it makes us wonder: how much do we ourselves withdraw into our own painful state of self-absorption?

THE SCIENCE OF AWAKENING

When we extend generosity to others, not only do we ease their pain, we also awaken—come out of our own isolation—in the process. There's a science to serving others.

Whenever we visit a big city we can stop and offer money to the homeless people we encounter on the street. So often we see people rushing around, trying to get where they are going. But when we take a moment to make an offering to someone in need, and have a human interaction, it changes the whole atmosphere of our mind and theirs. It takes us out of automatic pilot. Serving others is the antithesis of retreating into the self. It is an energetic shift that moves us toward the open and boundaryless state of interdependence.

Rinpoche often says we don't have to get rid of the self or ego when we do this. We don't have to change the basic makeup of our mind at all. We simply need to make ourselves big enough to include others in our wish for happiness rather than just focusing entirely on ourselves. In other words, the more we decentralize the self—the more we spread our wealth of love and care—the freer and bigger we become. We discover a happiness that is not reliant on the conditions and preferences of self-care.*

When we serve beings with all our might, our aspiration to

*Dzigar Kongtrül, *Light Comes Through: Buddhist Teachings on Awakening to Our Natural Intelligence* (Boston: Shambhala Publications, 2008).

benefit them shepherds us toward the bigger truth of interdependence. As our wisdom of the interdependent and the boundaryless nature of things increases, so does our compassion and inclination to serve. Do you see the relationship between these two? Without this bigger view, we would simply try to fix things in our limited, objectified world. And without the practice of service, we would have no way out of that world.

The science of awakening is not just a Buddhist principle. It is a shared experience that reflects the laws of cause and effect. When I listen to the news I am often struck by the stories I hear. People who experience great loss and suffering naturally look for ways to serve others. They move from "I am suffering" to "there is suffering," which inspires in them a longing to serve. The love that inspires this longing is the same love we all have when we stop focusing solely on ourselves and move toward the truth of interdependence.

"Best then," as my teacher says, "to become the keepers of our brothers and sisters." Best then, that they become the object of our understanding and love. Best then, that we care for them as our means to awaken to the great interdependence of things beyond self and other.

ENGAGEMENT

We often think of engagement as social activism. What we call "engaged Buddhism" is Buddhism that takes on a cause. But the Buddhist path, by its very nature, is a path of engagement. When we make ourselves big enough to include all beings in our love and care—when we accommodate everything—we fully engage the world. We are right there with everyone and everything else.

Our level of engagement doesn't necessarily depend upon the amount of social action we undertake. We can serve others while being totally disengaged and self-involved, in which case our actions will be puny. Or, we can be totally engaged while sitting alone in a small retreat hut. People who have done long retreats often talk about this experience. When they set their boundary at the beginning of retreat they feel isolated. There is a sense of trying to keep the world out. Later, a deep loneliness sets in. But instead of feeling depressed by this loneliness, they feel touched by a heartfelt sense of kinship with other beings, as if the entire universe of beings were sitting right beside them in their small hut.

Some people think that retreat practice is just another way to withdraw from the world, and I suppose it could be. But if we consider how much time we spend running around, distracted, thinking only of ourselves, perhaps it will lead us to wonder ... whether staying alone and reflecting deeply into the nature of things might actually be a brave and noble thing to do. I personally find solace in the fact that there are people in this world committed to this kind of wakefulness.

The point is that engagement happens when the artificial barriers between self and other, my retreat and the world outside, in and out, begin to fade. Engagement takes us beyond the extremes of complacency or trying to fix things, and demands the courage and presence of the Middle Way mind. The greatest kindness we have to offer others is to not withdraw into our self.

13

The Activity of Objectification

This is the game: the more self expands to include others, the more kindness, compassion, and insight we experience. The more fixed we get about things, the more confusion, emotional disturbance, and conflict we experience. Have you ever noticed that when you're angry at someone you always hold a narrow and static view of them? They are "the person who did . . ."

Attachment, jealousy, and aggression only function when we objectify things. That's why soldiers in combat are trained to hold static, negative images of "the enemy." How can we kill someone when we see his humanity? How can we hate someone when we see him face to face, when we know he is somebody's son, father, or brother?

How can we have attachment when we see the dimensionality of an object—when it becomes more than just "the thing we want"? In fact, the whole purpose of advertising is to get people to want something through presenting only one side of things. If someone were to say, "Hey, this is a really nice car. Look how slick it is. See how fast it goes. But it takes a lot of fuel, and you can be sure the dashboard will crack in a couple of years. Oh, and the electrical system sometimes breaks down after thirty thousand miles"—it would most likely reduce our attachment to buying that car.

When we objectify things, we don't think about the consequences of trying to obtain them: the tax consequences, the emotional consequences, the consequences they may have for others. When we see things in this limited way, we leave ourselves vulnerable to nothing but hassle, pain, and confusion. This example illustrates the dangers of ignorance—the ignorance of not being able to tolerate the interdependent and boundaryless nature of things.

THE BIG BANG

From within the fluid and ineffable state of boundarylessness, the knowing mind experiences a stirring . . . a discomfort of sorts. Somehow it's not enough to just rest in the boundaryless nature of this discomfort. The knower of this discomfort then acts, and leaves the open state to become the doer, or "subject." And what do subjects do? They define, seduce, wrestle with, and push away objects. And this dynamic exchange between subject and object creates a whole lot of friction and heat, which activates a big bang of sorts . . . And the whole world of objectification bursts into action.

The world as we commonly know it is simply the expression of this basic misunderstanding or intolerance of boundarylessness. This misunderstanding comes into play each moment we turn away from the fullness of experience to instead reach conclusions about things. As we proceed to either push things away or pull them closer to us, we are acting out the drama we call "our life." We traditionally call the energy behind this drama "karma."

Karma is a loaded word. Karma is popularly used to describe a sort of "divine plan" that includes its own system of punishment and reward. But the Sanskrit word karma simply means activity. What is the activity we are describing here? It is the activity of objectification. There is no Dr. Evil sitting in a large chair petting his cat and controlling our karma. There is no judge, no wise old man with a long white beard, no list of ethical "rights" and "wrongs." Karma doesn't predetermine anything. In fact, karma is just the movement of objectified experience. Karma is the natural, impersonal law of cause and effect. As long as we objectify things, we will continue to live in a world that follows the dictates of karma.

In this world, subjects run around trying to get what they want. They try to not get what they don't want. Sometimes they get what they want . . . but it turns out it is not what they wanted . . . especially when they shop online. Occasionally, thank goodness, subjects also encounter situations in which they get what they don't want but later on find out that it is what they wanted, after all.

But the point here is that there's a lot of preference in this world, a lot of fears and hopes, a lot of pushes and pulls with our thoughts and emotions, with people and material things. Conflict begins. War begins. More and more misunderstandings occur, which create an objectified universe, samsara . . . the universe that Nagarjuna described as "the most amazing spectacle of all."*

OTHER

The world that we objectify is a mythical and dreamlike existence, but it still has rules. And the savvier we get about these rules, the more skillfully we can function in our delusion—and even find a way out of it. In other words, it behooves us to understand the rules of karma because the way we respond to the world of things can create a big mess—or, it can create the causes and conditions of our awakening.

---

*Samsara ('khor ba) literally means "moving in circles" or "going around and around." It is the repeated process that arises from our continued tendency to leave the open state of boundarylessness and grasp at and push away objects. So why does Nagarjuna call it a "spectacle"? Because from the point of view of someone abiding in boundarylessness, like Nagarjuna, it is an elaborate and poignant misunderstanding.

The rules of karma work like this: the more fervently we create artificial boundaries in boundarylessness, the more we struggle in our realm of unfixable things. The more we expand to accommodate things, the softer the boundaries of self and other become, bringing us more in accord with boundarylessness. One approach keeps us in the dark; the other moves us out of darkness. One creates suffering; the other reveals the natural qualities of love, compassion, and insight that release as we awaken to interdependence. Sometimes we call this the creation of negative and positive karma. But understand that actions are only "positive" or "negative" by virtue of how they function in bringing us closer to a sense of well-being and the truth of boundarylessness. Other than the way they function, like all things, they posses no inherent or static truth.

From within the truth of thinglessness there is no karma, no negative or positive activities, because in boundarylessness, what does what to what? Who gets angry at or tries to benefit whom? Everything is a work in progress. The evidence is never all in. The data is incomplete. The more openness and curiosity we have about things, the more clarity and suppleness arises in the mind. Aggression and attachment lose their juice when we start to see the breadth and depth of things. We have moved away from a contracted icy state of seeing them as an enemy or a thing to get and moved toward the mysterious and watery truth of interdependence, where we know better than to reach definitive conclusions about anything.

I have said a lot about the Middle Way and going beyond the dualistic extremes of an objectified self and other. But curiously, when we function within our mythical world of things, it is "other" that brings us out of our hiding and leads us toward the bigger view— the view beyond all artificial boundaries.

14

Unspoken Agreements

If things are truly boundaryless then how do we explain the fact that we humans see things in a common way? We agree that money is paper, that it is better to chew with our mouths closed, and that we should stand in line at the post office. Sometimes we agree to be ignorant—for instance, in our agreement to pretend we're not going to die. And we agree that things are what we call them— we don't mix up our apples and oranges. We agree to navigate the world in this way together. Humans have all kinds of agreements: global, cultural, familial, and personal.

For instance, somewhere along the line, someone decided we should drive on the right side of the road in the United States. And down the center of these roads they painted yellow lines to divide the drivers going in opposite directions. They installed poles with changing red, green, and yellow lights in every intersection and spread the word that red means "stop," green means "go," and yellow means "proceed with caution"—in order to prevent accidents. We agree to this—most of the time—because we want to get to where we're going—and survive. And we trust that everyone else wants to survive, too. It's our unspoken driving pact.

Families also have pacts. As we grow up, our particular family's values shape our image of how things should be: for instance, what a marriage should look like or what a successful person might do. These values influence the many life decisions we make, such as what religion to follow or what ethical guidelines we should base our actions on. Such guidelines can support us, but sometimes they can be unhealthy. Sometimes we have to break these agreements just to grow.

THE AGREEMENT OF REALNESS

The most insidious agreement we make is that things are real, that we are real, and that the push and pull we have with the world of things is real, too. It is not only an agreement we have with others, it is the deep unspoken agreement we have with ourselves. In our quest for security we have decided to try to find ground in a world that is never fixed and always open to interpretation. We can say this decision is not completely conscious—but it is a decision, nonetheless. If we look around we may notice that everyone is guided by a sense of realness.

Yet what we agree upon as real or unreal is a little ambiguous. From the time we are small, we are told, for instance, that we had better floss, because our teeth are real; but, alas, we find out the tooth fairy is not. We believe our ideas and perceptions are real, but our dreams are not. Rocks must certainly be real, because they are heavy and dense, but ethereal things like mist or sea-foam bubbles—we're not sure. Emotions—they sure seem real, because they tend to overtake us when we have them. And all those unseen things that science talks about—like atoms—we kind of believe in those, because a lot of knowledgeable people tell us they are true. There are a lot of mixed messages. Can we find the dividing line between real and unreal? Plenty of people throughout history have pondered this.

Navigating "Thinglessness"

The fact that cultures or families make their own agreements proves that there's no inherent reality to our unspoken pacts. For instance, the people of India have organized their roads and driving laws in a way that is completely different from those in the United States. If you drive in India you can just do what you want—but you have to honk a lot to let everyone know you're there. And there is an unspoken agreement that the largest vehicle gets to go first: trucks before cars, cars before people (and, of course, cows before everything). Indians agree to relax and let everything loose. Indian people know how to navigate chaos, which creates an incredible order to life that we Westerners find so intriguing when we go there.

We see around us an unlimited variety of agreements, which suggest that they are all pretty arbitrary. In fact, the world that we objectify exists only upon agreement. There is no one way. There is no one way to be, no inherently correct driving system, no fixed way to live a life. At the same time, in order to live together we need consensus.

Don't Believe Everything You Think

We have a hard time wrapping our minds around boundaryless-ness. One of the most common confusions we have about the Middle Way is how to function in thinglessness. If no thing has a boundary, what prevents it all from just dissolving into boundaryless space? If the table is not real, where do I put my unreal cup?

In truth, the question of realness can't be answered by intellectual speculation. It is a simple question and can only be answered by direct experience. We can see, if we take the time to really look, that things change and shift, and we can't pin them down. Yet we manage to pay our phone bill, earn a living, and speak in a language that communicates what we think. There seems to be no real conflict between making agreements and knowing the boundaryless nature of things.

When I talk about boundarylessness, then, I am not holding the value of the world-of-agreements in question. Nor am I questioning the importance of our actions. What I am suggesting is that we question realness itself. Do we need to invest things with an objective realness in order for them to function?

Rinpoche put a large yellow and black bumper sticker on his retreat cabin door that reads, "Don't believe everything you think," just to remind anyone who enters not to take the world of things at face value. There's nothing far-reaching or esoteric about this instruction. It's simple. All we need to remember is that all things are thingless . . . yet every thing matters.

15

The Culture of Truth

Many years ago, in Nepal, when I was a new bride fumbling around trying to fit into my new Tibetan family, my mother-in-law gave me some advice that changed my view of spiritual practice.

But before I tell you what she said, I must explain that Kongtrül Rinpoche's mother, Mayum Tsewang Palden, was not an ordinary woman, but a seasoned Dharma* practitioner, a true yogini.† She wasn't casually tossing out some words. Her words came from experience, and this is what she said: "You don't have to become a Tibetan. You don't have to be an Ingie.‡ Just know your own mind."

These words of kindness pointed me in the direction of true practice. They took me beyond the foreign cultural forms I was wrestling with and helped me to overcome the complex and naive ideas I had about being a spiritual practitioner.

---

*(Tibetan, Ch'os) the teachings of the Buddha that lead to enlightenment.
†A yogini (Sanskrit; masculine root, *yogin*) is a term for a female meditation practitioner who has dedicated her life to spiritual attainment.
‡A Tibetan term for foreigners, specifically Westerners.

Basic Human Questions

As we study the Buddha's life, we see that all the questions he asked had to do with knowing the mind. He questioned the nature of thoughts and emotions; he wanted to know the causes and conditions for happiness and suffering; he wanted to get to the bottom of things. The path the Buddha taught addresses these basic human questions. They are not Tibetan questions, Indian questions, or American questions. They are beyond culture and beyond time.

The Buddha wasn't a social rebel. He didn't have the kind of presence that stirred things up. In fact, he brought peace to every situation, and his conduct was always compassionate and in accord with the language of the people. But the Buddha couldn't have been more radical. His truth was the boundaryless nature of being, which means he didn't adhere to the consensual agreement we all share about realness.

The Culture of Truth

In this world we live in, everything seems real: our cultural agreements seem real, our thoughts seem real, our anger and our fears seem real. The Buddha challenged the notion of realness through his inquiry, which revealed the boundaryless nature of things.

If we consider how entrenched we are in realness, how much we objectify experience, we will understand the value of the Buddha's wisdom. Without it how could we possibly break free from the powerful misunderstandings we have about mind and reality? How could we dismantle our habit of running from the full and boundaryless nature of things? How could we come to know our own mind?

When, like the Buddha, we begin to question that things may not be as they seem, we join a lineage of people—a culture of truth—who aspire to transcend a limited view of reality. This is exciting, don't you think? Envision living in a culture not based upon fixed views. Imagine activities that do not stem from "I am"—not even "I am a Buddhist" or "I am a member of the culture of truth" or "I am Indian, Tibetan, or American." Since the time of the Buddha, the culture of looking beyond the appearance of things has brought freedom to its citizens.

Explaining Dharma to Ourselves

Having said this, some questions remain: What do we make of all the elaborate Buddhist imagery we encounter? The foreign words? The cultural nuances? How do they relate to our basic human questions? What do they have to do with knowing the mind?

To enter the culture of truth doesn't mean we must dismiss the wisdom of any culture or tradition. For instance, I feel touched when I think of the spirit in which the great Tibetan kings brought the Dharma to Tibet from India. The Dharma king Songtsen Gampo sent emissaries to the noble land of India to devise a written language based on Sanskrit that would accurately express the meaning of the Dharma. He did this with tenderness for the source of the teachings—the teachings that would eventually awaken the many yogis and yoginis of Tibet. We can appreciate the way our wisdom lineage came down to us—in a Zen way, a Tibetan way, or an Indian way. We should be attentive, however, to not turn this appreciation into a dismissal of the culture we grew up in. We simply need to discern which values support our path—such as generosity, kindness, and patience—and which do not. Whichever lineage of the teachings we encounter helps us to fine-tune our ability to be discerning and make clear choices about our spiritual development.

Because the Dharma teachings speak directly to our own experience, how foreign could they be? And how native are our own cultural values and ideas, anyway? We were born naked and our parents dressed us in the culture we grew up in, so in a sense, nothing is native to us, until we make it personal and it serves us in some way.

When the teachings themselves start to seem foreign or unfamiliar we must come back to the culture of truth. We can talk about a new American Buddhism, or a modern Buddhist culture—but what is new about the mind? What is new about happiness, suffering, compassion, or liberation? So the question we need to ask is: how is the Dharma not foreign?

The pursuit of this question is a personal process, and how we do it is up to us. But as we begin to ask this question, we will see the teachings animate us, spur us on, wake us up, and come to life in us. Then we will know that it's not only how the Dharma is explained to us that is important, but how we explain it to ourselves. This is our work.

16

Enjoy the Feast

When our habitual tendency to objectify things relaxes, we can see the truth of boundarylessness. We call boundarylessness a "truth" because when we strip away everything extraneous to the nature of things—all the exaggeration, denial, unspoken agreements, and cultural values—this is what we see. We can say that the world we objectify is a truth, too, simply because we do experience the pain and pleasure of the world, stubbing our toe and so forth. Fair enough. In fact there is some scholarly debate over whether or not the world of things deserves to be called a truth. But as we have discussed, just because we experience something doesn't mean it has parameters; it doesn't mean that we can reach conclusions about it or find in it even a trace of realness.

The great scholar of the Middle Way, Chandrakirti,* had something to say about all of this.

*Chandrakirti was a renowned seventh-century Indian master known for his exposition on the Middle Way teachings of Nagarjuna's *Verses on the Middle Way* (*Mulamadhyamaka-karikas*). Chandrakirti's commentary, *Introduction to the Middle Way* (Sanskrit, *Madhyamakavatara*), is one of the most revered and influential texts among scholars of the Middle Way.

He argued that because we can't find realness in the world of things, there can really only be one truth, the truth of boundary-lessness. I like his way of looking at things.

One truth doesn't mean everything is one. We've gone over that. If everything were one, what would account for the staggering variety of appearances we see around us? One truth means that every thing is equal in its boundaryless nature. So whether things are man-made or untouched by men, organic or sprayed, wood or plastic, mineral or chemical, pleasing or painful, clean or dirty, when we examine them we can't find their parameters. In this way, all things are equal in nature.

ENJOY THE FEAST

When we bring the understanding that all things are equal into the realm of practice, we traditionally call that experience "one taste." We have formal ways of practicing one taste in the context of the Vajrayana* tradition. In our community, members gather twice monthly to do feast practice. The emphasis of feast practice is to experience and enjoy the full and boundaryless nature of things as "one taste." A segment of this practice calls for a ritual food offering. The students prepare large trays of fruits and various desirable foods, which they offer to the buddhas and bodhisattvas. Then the text instructs us to "Enjoy the feast."

What an easy practice, right? Au contraire. With all our desires and preferences, how do we truly enjoy food? And not only that:

---

*The Vajrayana (Sanskrit), or "indestructible vehicle," is the most developed stage in the evolution of Buddhist practice. It consists mostly of oral and secret instructions passed down from teacher to student. The practices of the Vajrayana are the most expedient path to awakening, because they don't aim to purify the mind and its confused world of objectification, but rather they take all experience onto the path without the preferences and judgments of ordinary thinking. The practice of one taste, as described here, exemplifies this approach.

with all our habits of objectification, how do we enjoy food with one taste? This practice, in the beginning, throws most people into a tizzy . . . Does one taste mean we should cast all discernment out the window and pretend all food tastes the same? Does it mean that because we have our eye on the Oreos we should counteract that by modestly taking an apple off the tray as it goes by, in order to suppress our desire? Or does it mean we can indulge in anything we want? And what if we don't want to eat the Twinkie on our plate?

As you can see, one taste doesn't work in the world we objectify. The world of objectification is riddled with preferences: the tug-of-war with our wants and not-wants. The understanding we cultivate through doing this practice brings us to a bigger view of experience—an experience free of such confusions.

Now laugh if you want, but the truth of even an Oreo is that it is thingless, elusive, unfindable, and infinite. Oreos too are part of the great interdependence of things. So before we just dive into our plate of Oreos, why not take a moment and wonder: How did this Oreo get here? Who was involved? Where did all the ingredients that went into making this Oreo come from? What did the sugarcane field look like? What kind of climate does sugarcane grow in? What kind of elements does it require to grow? Who cut the sugarcane and how was it processed? What kind of tools did they use? Who makes those artificial flavors and colorings? How do they get the cream in the middle without breaking the chocolate part? And what about the truck that ships the packages to the store and the fuel that makes it possible—who was involved in that?

All of a sudden, an Oreo looks considerably different. It's not just this round little bite-sized thing anymore. In fact, it has no boundary. When we have a feast, we celebrate the fullness and abundance of boundarylessness. We enjoy the experience of knowing things without objectifying them or defining them in a limiting or constricted way. This is true enjoyment.

Enjoyment beyond Preference

True enjoyment has nothing to do with pleasure as opposed to pain, yummy as opposed to yucky, good as opposed to bad. It is the experience of including and appreciating the magical and unfindable nature of all appearance—even the appearances that challenge us, like illness or depression.

Rinpoche once referred to depression as "dakini bliss." What does that mean?

In traditional Buddhist iconography, a dakini is depicted as a female wisdom being. But she also has a subtler manifestation. The dakini refers to the elemental nature of all things. So dakini bliss refers to the experience of enjoying the boundaryless nature of all things. When we don't objectify depression—or any other experience, such as food—we encounter its true mode of existence, naked, profound, and infinite. Seeing the boundaryless truth of things is bliss, because it liberates us from the struggle with our wants and not-wants, and the hopes and fears that come from our preferences. Enjoying the bliss of the dakinis is the Vajrayana practice of one taste, and it takes us beyond the limits of our vegan-hood, our organic-hood, or our I-want- or don't-want-hood.

I suspect some questions may arise here: If we rest in the boundaryless nature of one taste, does that mean we dismiss our ability to discern? Does enjoying the bliss of the dakinis mean we have to reduce the copious display of experience to a bland and flavorless neutrality? Does it mean we should eat all the Twinkies even though they might give us a stomachache? Certainly not. Actually, there are many different-colored dakinis: red ones, green ones, and yellow ones. In other words, infinite expression is also ours to enjoy. And as we navigate the world of infinite expression, our ability to discriminate makes it possible for us to lead a sane life in the service of others. This ability to discern is one of our greatest gifts. The point is to discern and enjoy the variety of things with a bigger view. Our mind has the ability to do both without contradiction.

Let's look at the mechanics of vision, in order to understand the idea of "bigger view." We have a peripheral vision and a focused vision. We can, for instance, see a vast and open sky as well as the clouds, birds, and airplanes that move through it. We can see big and small at the same time. These two abilities function together, interdependently. The more we relax our peripheral vision, the clearer our focus. And the less we strain to see details, the wider the lens. This should be fairly obvious. When we soften and relax, we function better in all areas of our life. If our eyes are relaxed, they naturally pick up images without our having to do anything, the way forms reflect on a clear and placid lake.

The traditional Vajrayana texts explain the two wisdoms of the buddhas: the wisdom that sees the boundaryless nature of things and the wisdom that knows the multitude or variety of appearances and how they arise and fall away through causes and conditions. These two wisdoms connect us to the wealth of the world and our ability to enjoy it.

While enjoying the boundaryless and infinite expression of things, we often hear the great beings exclaim: *"Emaho!"* "Isn't it amazing!" I reckon it's because they no longer struggle with things. For them, all things are simply part of the great feast of experience . . . simply there to enjoy.

17

Digesting Experience

As we study the life of the Buddha we realize that he asked basic human questions about happiness, suffering, freedom from suffering, compassion, interdependence, death, life, and the nature of things. But if we were to pare all these questions down into one essential question, we might come up with something like this: how do we take in the world of "things"? That is, how do we process the continuous stream of occurrences that arise in our life? How do we digest experience?

When we eat, we ingest, process, and eliminate food. Our bodies use food as fuel for life and eliminate what is no longer useful. It would be great to say that we digested our experience with such ease. But there is something about being human that doesn't come naturally to us. We can't seem to take experience in, let it work on us, and then let it go. Either we refuse to ingest experience—in which case our life doesn't nourish us—or we hold on to experience until it turns toxic. The struggle we have with experience gives us mental and emotional indigestion. Our relationship to experience is all about fighting the world, rejecting the unwanted, trying to fix things, and creating strategies for living around experience.

Someone once asked Dzigar Kongtrül Rinpoche if he was afraid to die. He answered that he was more afraid of living his life despite himself. What I think he meant here is that life presents itself to us, but we'd often prefer to live in fantasy. We'd rather not ingest our experience—eat our life—in the way it presents itself to us. We'd rather be someone else, somewhere else, having a different experience. We may wonder: Why should we take in the fullness of life? That means we have to take in sadness, uncertainty, and fear. Why can't we just take in whatever makes us comfortable? Yet this very attitude toward our experience points to the struggle we have with our world.

There is no life without experience. Life and experience are synonymous. Life just unfolds, so we can't reject experience the way we can food. But we can fight it tooth and nail. And this is what I am talking about here. We can turn on the news and not really hear the names of the soldiers who died in Iraq that day. We can blame others for all the conflict in our lives and never learn to self-reflect or resolve a situation creatively. We can vent our emotions all over the place—and in doing so we may imagine that we are responding directly to life. But do we really let life in this way? Or, in reacting, are we keeping our life at bay? And if we keep our life at a distance, how can it nourish us? How can it move through us? How can we absorb it and let it work its magic?

When we look at any of the accomplished lineage masters of our tradition, we never see them struggle with conceptual or emotional indigestion in the way we do. They take in all experience with one taste, utilizing everything as food for realization. Experience moves through their bodies, through their awareness, and nourishes them. The great masters are always "eating," and whatever they eat generates boundless energy, intelligence, and compassion. It turns out that practice accomplishment is nothing more than learning to be natural with our experience—not unlike the body's natural ability to digest food.

As practitioners we might wonder: what would it be like to be so natural, so ordinary? We should ask this question again and again, because it does away with all the fluffy fantasies we have about spirituality; all this waiting for something special to happen; all the excitement we feel when something unexplainable occurs; all the disappointment we encounter when nothing special comes our way. It directs us to the point of practice: finding contentment in being fully human, natural, and ordinary.

18

The Mark of Non-Creating

The first practice instruction Rinpoche ever gave to me was: "Don't create." He told me, "Leave your mind in its natural state—don't do anything. When thoughts and sensations arise, just let them arise. When they fall away, just let them fall away. Don't try to manipulate them." Then he went to Tibet for six months . . .

My teacher's instruction—"Don't create"—presented me with a koan: If the world of our creation occurs through the activity of objectification, what happens when we stop objectifying? If we just let things be, rather than trying to manipulate, embellish, or suppress them, what's our role in the creation of our lives?

This kind of questioning began my personal investigation into the nature of things—an investigation that continues to this day and is one of the reasons I am writing this book. When we explore things, we have many adventures along the way. Let me tell you about one of mine.

Oh No, Not That Thing

Many years ago I traded in my distracted, tightly scheduled city life for a life in the mountains of Crestone, Colorado. Crestone is a vast and lonely place. It doesn't feed the habitual appetite for doing. In fact, the only thing it does provide is a lot of space. And so, during my first months here, I got depressed . . .

Actually I don't know if I could even call it depression. It wasn't the lethargic, purposeless feeling I have heard others talk about. It was a "buzzy" kind of pain that wasn't sleepy or dull. Instead, it shouted, "Wake up!" and I couldn't get away from it no matter what I did. This pain caught hold of my whole body so that when I tried to move, everything hurt. I pressed my seized-up body into a chair and sat there without moving or doing anything for the most part of each day . . . until the sun got lower in the sky and the light softened and the hard edge of pain thawed, bringing me to a deep state of peace. Then I woke up abruptly before dawn, to begin again.

Every morning I would wake up to confront this thing. And every day for over a month I had the opportunity to face my inability to fix this thing and to function in a familiar way. Truly, it was one of the greatest opportunities of my life. Trying to create a comfortable situation for myself didn't work. Trying to distract myself from it, manipulate it, or reach conclusions about it didn't help. But the more I gave up trying to fix it, the more I could relax in the eye of the storm.

What was this thing? I'll never know. Who can find something so slippery and insubstantial, so deep and elusive? What mattered is that I began to appreciate the natural energy and vitality of my own mind, and I didn't want to escape it. In fact, I felt alive, and the eye of the storm became the place I wanted to be.

I often recall Rinpoche's instruction: "Don't create." Where was he directing me? It turns out he was guiding me toward an experience that was not created through objectification—an experience beyond exaggeration and denial. In short, he was pointing me to the natural uncontrived truth of boundarylessness and its rich creative expression.

THE MUSE

In the family I grew up in, "creative" people were always considered the most interesting. Art, music, and literature were highly valued expressions of a society. Creativity was a good thing. So "not-creating" challenged my newly emerging understanding of what practice might be . . . and I had to rethink creativity in general.

People in the world of art, music, and literature always talk about "the muse." Who is she, anyway? I'm pretty sure she's not the voice that comes in and says, "I before e except after c." I don't think she tells us what to do, and I'm not even sure she inspires us. I'm beginning to think that genuine creativity emerges when we take a step back and stop creating—stop doing. I think the muse is this unhindered boundaryless creativity itself.

Rinpoche studies art with Yahne Le Toumelin—an artist who paints in a way that is freeing, nonconceptual, and expressive. Her method requires the painter to move with and watch the expression of texture and color unfolding on the canvas without passing judgments such as "beautiful" or "ugly," "good" or "bad." The discipline of this approach becomes simply to stop creating and let things be.

If the painter clings to his or her preferences, Le Toumelin encourages the artist to continue working until he or she can allow natural creativity to come through. When this happens, the painter reaches what Rinpoche calls "the mark of non-creating"—a state of natural creativity where the artist has stepped out of his or her own way. When all fixations are exhausted, the painter puts down the brush without trying to improve upon or manipulate the final result. The process I watch Rinpoche go through yields paintings that embody an uncontrived naturalness. And that naturalness speaks to everyone who observes his work.

We have probably all heard stories of great writers and artists whose work represents the creativity that emerges when we don't succumb to the ordinary concepts of how things should be. Picasso used to blot out whole paintings when he became attached to images. In writing, when we cling to a word, phrase, or paragraph it inhibits the flow of surprises we enjoy and learn so much from. Writing often works best when we write about what we don't know . . . rather than what we do.

Where does this flow of surprises come from? As Rinpoche says, we often think of creativity as belonging to the artist. But in a larger sense, he says, the universe of appearances and possibilities arises naturally without our creating anything. It is not the product of hammer and nail. The mountains, the trees, the sun, and the moon have arisen without our involvement. Everything we have been and everything we have known since we stepped into this world arises from this natural boundaryless creativity.*

TRUST

How we unlock natural creativity in our experience is not limited to art. It points to a way of being. It points to the spirit of not-knowing, to the koan, to tolerating thinglessness, to a mind free of conclusions, to the Middle Way mind that knows the boundaryless nature of things. This way of being gives us the freedom to experience and engage mind and the world in the most direct and alive way.

Not creating takes some trust—the kind of trust the Buddha had when he gave up all views and sat beneath the Bodhi Tree. And from this viewless space, the Buddha came to understand

*Dzigar Kongtrül, *Natural Vitality*. (Crestone, Colo.: Sarasvati Publishing, 2007).

the nature of things, which enabled him to articulate the path of wisdom—the pilgrimage that leads us from misunderstanding to enlightenment. Now this is not something some ordinary Joe could patch together. It is truly an expression of uncontrived brilliance.

19

The Perfect Teacher

When I think about my teacher, Dzigar Kongtrül Rinpoche, I feel deep appreciation, love and loneliness, sadness and warmth, all at the same time. But if you were to ask me who or what my teacher truly is, I couldn't tell you.

I've spent a lot of time trying to understand him.* But every time I think, "I've got him now—I know who he is," I run into problems. The teacher, like all things, is beyond definition or objectification. If we can keep our relationship to the teacher an open question, we will experience the fullness of his kindness and find our way into true practice.

THE TEACHER KOAN

In the Vajrayana texts it says, "Always see the teacher as a perfect Buddha." This is a challenging statement, don't you think? How

---

*I have used the male pronoun here because my teacher is a man. But you can substitute the female pronoun if you have a female teacher.

can we see anything as "perfect" when our minds are confused—when we move about in the limited world of objectification?

The world we objectify is a world based upon fantasies, wants and not-wants—a world where the ego does everything it can to survive. This world, by its very nature, never reaches a state of perfection. It never satisfies or brings lasting happiness—it always disappoints. So if we look at the teacher in this ordinary way, he will disappoint us, too.

When we enter the spiritual path we have a lot of fantasies about what a teacher should be: a father, a superhero, a monk, a perfect Buddha. We may expect certain behavioral traits in our teacher, such as political correctness. We may expect lightness and humor or prefer seriousness and piety. We may want attention or independence. But generally we want a savior, and we want to be saved in a way that is comfortable for us. If we hold on to these fantasies, the teacher has a lot to live up to. It's a lot to ask of another human being—an impossible demand, really.

Commonly when we think of the teacher as a perfect Buddha, we are just thinking of this limited image we have of him—what we want him to be. Our idea of perfect is forced and contrived, not experienced. This is because the way we see the teacher is not perfect. So when our perfect teacher does something we don't understand, we have a hard time maintaining our grand and static view of him: perfect falls apart.

When this happens we start to see the teacher as an ordinary guy, and we have to fake our devotion* a little—pump it up, so to

---

*Devotion comes from a deep sense of appreciation for someone or something that has benefited us. On the Vajrayana path this appreciation plays an important role in awakening. Through devotion, we give up the objectified view we have of ourselves and our world in order to have a bigger experience, although sometimes we are not sure what that bigger experience might be. Sometimes devotion arises without deliberate effort. Other times we need to cultivate devotion through reflecting on the teacher as the source of the teachings, on his kindness or qualities. But it is only when we experience the freedom and warmth of the practice directly that a natural or uncultivated devotion wells up from within. So in the end, devotion to the teacher is directly related to the relationship we have with our own practice.

speak. Meanwhile, we wonder what went wrong. We wonder: Is the teacher failing or am I just a horrible student? Where did my devotion go? Why can't I be like the disciples I read about in the texts? Why can't I see the teacher as a perfect Buddha? We may even start to doubt the possibility of liberation altogether. We jump back and forth between fantasy and doubt in this way. This big dilemma comes from having a small view of the teacher.

Please understand, I am not saying that our teachers don't have extraordinary qualities. But the point is that we can't truly know the teacher through seeing him in this limited way.

HOOK AND RING

The Vajrayana texts sometimes describe the relationship between the teacher and student through the analogy of hook and ring. This metaphor begins to mess with our idea of an objectified "perfect" by elucidating the interdependent relationship between teacher and student. If the hook refers to the teacher's ability to take hold of the student in order to lead him or her to enlightenment, this analogy suggests that we, as students, must become a ring. What does it mean to become a ring?

The most illustrious example of a ring was the Buddha himself. And this is interesting because the Buddha never had a Buddhist teacher. But when we talk about becoming a ring, we start to get at the attitude, vision, and spirit a practitioner needs in order to wake up. And these the Buddha had in spades.

The Buddha taught us that liberation is grounded in understanding basic human challenges. There is nothing mystical about liberation, and, in fact, he showed us how to go about it. We've watched the Buddha look deeply into the causes and conditions of suffering rather than turning away from it. We've discussed his dissatisfaction with the world of things and how he burned with the desire to find an answer to the human condition. And we've seen how this dissatisfaction and his longing for truth kept him awake and guided him to enlightenment. All of this illustrates the spirit of the practice—the practice of becoming a ring.

If you were to ask what touches me most about my teacher, I would have to say his honesty, bravery, and his profound dissatisfaction with the self and all its wants and not-wants. Disillusionment with the world of things creates a little sadness—a little distrust—and at times I've seen him struggle. So often we think of this kind of humanness as a weakness or a fault. But in fact, to be fully human takes courage—the courage to face life instead of living in fantasy.

Without this longing to see beyond the world of self and all its fantasies, what role would the teacher actually play in our lives? We would continue in our usual attempt to create a semblance of security for ourselves and would necessarily have to resist any advice or instruction he had to offer.

If we didn't share in the teacher's vision to liberate the mind through self-reflection, we would only have two ways to view the teacher—and both these ways would keep the teacher at a safe distance: we would either find fault and weakness in the teacher, or, conversely, we would perceive the teacher as living in a totally different world—a sublime reality inaccessible from our own. But what could such a teacher do for us? He would be too divine for us to understand. What would be so impressive about this kind of teacher? What could we learn from such a person? What kind of example would he be? How could such a person help us work with our basic human challenges: suffering, old age, sickness, and death?

Milarepa was a Tibetan *yogin* well known for his unwavering devotion to his teacher and for his many years of solitary meditation retreat. In his biography, a disciple sings Milarepa's praises by saying, in effect, "You are so accomplished, so sublime, it is certain that you have been a Buddha from the very start. We humans cannot even conceive of the extent of your perseverance and devotion, let alone practice it ourselves." Milarepa responds to him by saying, "Although your praise of me springs from your devotion, there is no greater impediment to your practice. The fault lies in not recognizing the power and efficacy of the Dharma and the true nature of the achievement of great yogis, whose attainment is due especially to single-minded devotion to meditation."*

This is a profound instruction. Here, Milarepa points out the true job of the student. It's easy to put the teacher on a pedestal, as this particular student did. And it's easy to find faults in the teacher, too. It's easy because this way we don't have to do the work—the work of becoming a ring. But what's not so easy is to see the teacher beyond our preferences and fantasies—beyond objectification. That takes some depth, some vision.

Teacher and student are not mutually exclusive—they share an intimate relationship of interdependence. They are hook and ring. And so it is that if we understand the nature of the ring, we will naturally understand the nature of the hook. Until then, we will never truly meet the teacher.

MEETING THE TEACHER

It may sound as if the topic here is the teacher, but our investigation of the teacher really just throws us back on ourselves. In many respects, the path of becoming a ring is a lonely one. We think, as we do in all relationships, that now that we have a teacher we don't have to be alone—finally, the loneliness gap is filled. But we find, in the end, that we're lonelier than ever. And our loneliness is accentuated by knowing that separation is inevitable and that liberation is truly up to us.

This loneliness we experience is not a bad thing. Acquainting ourselves with loneliness comes from giving up our fantasies and

---

*Paraphrased from *The Life of Milarepa*, translated by Lobsang P. Lhalungpa (London: Penguin Arkana Publications, 1992), pp. 144–45.

is a necessary step on the path. In fact, loneliness serves as our companion on the path—that is, until we truly meet the teacher. Let me explain.

In the Vajrayana literature there is a recurring pattern, a drama of sorts. It takes place each time a teacher is about to leave this world. At that time, the teacher passes the heart essence of the lineage to a disciple. In the Nyingma* lineage, this tradition begins with Garab Dorje† and continues for many generations of practitioners to the great adept who brought Buddhism to Tibet, Guru Rinpoche, and his principle disciple, Yeshe Tsogyal.‡

The scenario goes like this: Guru Rinpoche is about to leave this world, and his disciple Yeshe Tsogyal begins to lament. She tears out her hair, bangs her limbs against the rocks, and cries out, "How can you leave us? How can you be so cruel?" This goes on for some time until Guru Rinpoche drops down from the sky and sings her a song about impermanence. "You knew this would happen," he says, "this is the nature of things."

But this doesn't pacify Yeshe Tsogyal in the least. Again, she begins to lament. She begs the guru to stay. She beats her limbs against the rocks until they bleed, until Guru Rinpoche reemerges.

---

*The Nyingma tradition (rNying ma), or "Old Translation School," is the oldest of the four major schools of Tibetan Buddhism. It was founded on the first translations of Buddhist scriptures from Sanskrit into Tibetan in the eighth century.

†Garab Dorje (dga' rab rdo rje) was born at the turn of the Common Era. He is known as the first human lineage holder of the Dzogpa Chenpo, or Great Perfection, teachings—the pinnacle of the Vajrayana tradition. He transmitted these teachings to his retinue of exceptional beings, including his chief disciple, Manjushrimitra. Padmasambhava is also said to have received transmission of the Dzogpa Chenpo teachings directly from Garab Dorje. He is especially known for his composition "Three Words That Strike the Vital Point" (tshig gsum ngad du brdegs).

‡Yeshe Tsogyal (ye-shes mtsho-rgyal), born in the eighth century, was the consort of the great Indian adept Guru Padmasambhava, who was responsible for establishing the Buddhadharma in Tibet. Yeshe Tsogyal was his principle disciple and became a master in her own right, guiding countless beings to liberation. She is highly revered as a female Buddha in Tibet.

But this time he drops a small casket, the size of a thumbnail, down from the sky. The casket contains the heart essence of the teachings, the nyingthig.*

Once the disciple holds the casket in her hands she relaxes, stops crying, and finally understands the nature of the whole relationship.†

When the disciple receives the casket she receives the blessings—the true meaning of practice. We can say the casket is a metaphor for the practice penetrating our experience, also known as liberation. And what is liberation? It is the world beyond objectification. When the practice penetrates the mind—even if it is only a moment of *bodhicitta*, a moment of seeing the boundaryless nature of things, a moment of faith—we become the ring. Hook and ring, teacher and student, come together.

Until this happens, there will always be a loneliness to the path. We have a teacher, but he can't make us happy. He can't take away our suffering or experience our mind for us. There's a loneliness in realizing it's up to us, that we have to confront old age, sickness, and death alone. Our pain is our own. The teacher can't fix it. No one can.

---

*The *nyingthig* (*snying thig*), or "heart essence" teachings, refers to the pith instruction section of the Great Perfection. In *The Precious Treasury of the Basic Space of Phenomena*, Kunchyen Longchenpa (Longchen Rabjam) describes the *nyingthig* teachings in this way: "Once one has reached the summit of a majestic mountain, one can see the valleys below all at once, while from the valleys one cannot see what it is like at the summit. Similarly, *ati* (another word for Dzogpa Chenpo), the vajra heart essence, is the pinnacle spiritual approach and sees what is meaningful in all others, while the lower approaches cannot see its ultimate meaning. Therefore, it is the pinnacle, the peak experience, which is spontaneously present" (Junction City, Calif.: Padma Publishing, 2004), p. 53.

†For a detailed account of the transmission from Padmasambhava to Yeshe Tsogyal, see Gyalwa Changchub and Namkhai, *Lady of the Lotus-Born: The Life and Enlightenment of Yeshe Tsogyal* (Boston: Shambhala Publications, 1999), pp. 137–46. For a more detailed account of the lineage transmission that begins with Garab Dorje to Manjushrimitra, Shrisimha, Jnanastura and Vimalamitra, see Nyoshul Khen Rinpoche, *A Marvelous Garland of Rare Gems: Biographies of Masters of Awareness in the Dzogchen Lineage* (Junction City, Calif.: Padma Publishing, 2005) or Tulku Thondrup, *Masters of Meditation and Miracles* (Boston: Shambhala Publications, 1996).

If we don't do the work of becoming the ring, we can serve the teacher night and day and never meet him. In the same way, we can sit on a cushion twelve hours a day without truly practicing, or we can stay in retreat for a lifetime but accomplish little. This is possible.

But when we truly meet the teacher, a profound appreciation wells up from within. It is like waking up to a vast ocean of kindness. The teacher has served as our example. He has shown us the way out of confusion by imparting personal advice and teachings to us. In essence, he has directed us to our own innate wisdom. And it is through this wisdom that we know him.

But there is more. When we meet the perfect teacher we see everything as perfect. This is because we see the world beyond our habitual objectification of it—we see the infinite and boundaryless nature of things. This is the fruit that comes from this special relationship . . . there is nothing else like it. But until we realize the true meaning of perfect, until we become the ring, the teacher will just be waiting, and waiting, and waiting . . .

20

Beyond "Blindism" and "Doubtism"

Tilopa, the renowned Indian meditation master, put his disciple Naropa through various trials to test and increase his faith, such as having him jump off cliffs and stick splinters of wood under his fingernails. After each incident Tilopa would miraculously revive Naropa's broken body.* And the Tibetan adept Marpa had his student Milarepa build huge monuments, which Milarepa had to tear down and re-erect for years before Marpa gave him even a single teaching.† These two illustrious disciples, Naropa and

---

*Tilopa (988–1069) was responsible for developing the Mahamudra method, a set of spiritual practices that greatly accelerates the process of awakening. He is known for transmitting these teachings to his principle disciple, Naropa, by hitting him on the head with his sandal. Naropa (956–1041) was an Indian scholar, yogi, mystic, and monk. He was also the teacher of Marpa the translator. Both Tilopa and Naropa are important figures in the Kagyu lineage of Tibetan Buddhism. You can find a concise account of this story in Patrul Rinpoche, *The Words of My Perfect Teacher*, 2nd ed. (Boston: Shambhala Publications, 1998), pp. 157–59.

†Lhodak Marpa Choski Lodos (1012–1097), affectionately known as Marpa the translator, was a Tibetan Buddhist teacher credited for bringing the transmission of many Buddhist texts to Tibet from India. He was also a householder, farmer, scholar, and teacher. He is best

Milarepa, exemplify the diligence and faith required to achieve liberation in the Buddhist Vajrayana tradition.

Yet we probably have questions about these extreme expressions of devotion. Do these stories suggest we should put our discerning intelligence aside and simply do what our teacher asks? Does it mean we should believe whatever we hear because the teachings say so? Rather than feeling inspired by such examples we start to question our faith.

Faith is an important yet illusive topic on the spiritual path—but what is "faith," exactly? If we don't investigate the true meaning of faith we will approach our practice either without discernment and personal vision or else with suspicion and skepticism. In other words, we will waffle back and forth between what Rinpoche calls "blindism" and "doubtism."

Blindism has a whole lot of "shoulds": "The tradition says I should, the teacher says I should, a practitioner should, my practice should, I should . . ." Where do all these shoulds come from? Blindism comes with a big assumption—mainly that we can't trust our own discernment, even though we have already chosen blindly to trust all those shoulds that seem to keep coming our way. Blindism makes us forget that we entered the spiritual path in the first place through relying upon our own discernment. We saw an opportunity and moved toward it. Now, having found the teachings, do we just lay our discriminating wisdom aside and passively await liberation? Do we just let shoulds navigate our ship? Or do we actively participate?

It's amazing what human beings can put up with, but we can only go along blindly for so long. Eventually, we fall into doubtism: "How does this practice relate to my life? Why isn't it work-

---

known through the accounts of his closest disciple, Milarepa. Both Marpa and Milarepa are central to the development of the Kagyu lineage of Tibetan Buddhism. You can find a more detailed account of this story in The Words of My Perfect Teacher (pp. 160–65) or The Life of Milarepa, translated by Lobsang P. Lhalungpa (London: Penguin Arkana Publications, 1992).

ing? Maybe I'm not cut out for this. Do thoughts ever settle down? Maybe I'm just a bad student. Could it be that the teachings just don't apply to my life? And as for my teacher, he seems ordinary to me. Enlightenment is obviously a myth . . ." Doubtism has its own assumptions. It assumes that it has already figured out, at least to some extent, how things are, so self-reflection and curiosity come to a standstill. Meanwhile, doubt revels in its own cleverness. But it's not nearly as clever as it thinks, because it gives us nowhere to go, which means it prevents us from learning anything new.

Blindism and doubtism reflect a deep dilemma we often have with ourselves. We want to be "good," but we're not sure how to carry that out in the context of our full humanness: our discontentment, our confusion, our hopes and fears, our wants and not-wants. In other words, we can't reconcile the shoulds and the doubts with our own sense of clarity and practice. We can't seem to access a greater intelligence beyond either blindism or doubtism. When this is so, how can we trust our own discernment?

THE HOTNESS OF FIRE

In truth, what good is faith without discernment? Is it even possible? In order to have faith we have to trust ourselves. Who else decides what path to take or what to have faith in? Who experiences the benefits of faith and the limits of blindism and doubtism? Who wants happiness and freedom from suffering? We do.

Buddhism takes a practical stance on all of this. The Buddha recognized our basic instinct for happiness as the seed of discerning intelligence. With the support of favorable causes and conditions, we can rely on discernment to guide us in a positive direction.

"Causes and conditions" in this case means the wisdom of the teachings. The teachings incite us to bring our own natural intelligence—our instinct for happiness—together with the wisdom of the path. They summon us to put this wisdom into effect, see if it brings welfare and happiness, and if it does, then put it to use. This takes engagement and vision. We've seen how the Buddha combined instinct, wisdom, and personal investigation . . . and he did it with passion, insight, creativity, and flair.

This process of personal investigation engenders a childlike wonder, in the company of which blindism and doubtism have no place. Blindism and doubtism have none of the agility, creativity, or spunk of wonderment. Wonderment instigates a state of continuous engagement, a mind free of assumptions and shoulds, an ignorance-free zone of sorts.

When we get beyond the myopic states of blindism and doubtism, we can see the whole game board, but we also see the pieces, how they move together and affect each other. We see, for instance, that self-absorption leads to suffering, while loving-kindness leads to freedom. We see the limits of objectifying things and the bravery that comes from bearing witness to our lives. We see how the teacher supports our awakening. It turns out that the activity of wonderment is a dynamic process of exploration that gives way to clear seeing.

At some point when we are young, someone is likely to tell us that fire is hot. But until we touch fire for the first time and burn our hand, we don't have a personal relationship to its hotness. After that experience, however, we have unwavering faith in its hotness. The burning sensation of fire is an experience that stays with us for a lifetime, because it is powerful and direct. I suspect it was this kind of faith—the kind of discernment and confidence that comes from seeing how things work—that spurred on the heroic meditators of the past.

WHAT'S YOUR PLAN?

So let's get back to those famous meditators. What were they really up to? Like so many other practitioners, I always wondered about their motivation and faith. One day, finally, I asked Rinpoche if these fervent disciples we read about in the Vajrayana texts—the ones we revere so highly—followed their teacher's instructions blindly. And he answered, "No. They knew exactly what they were doing."

Regardless of how extreme, arbitrary, or colorful jumping off a cliff may seem to us, for these disciples it was part of a bigger plan—a plan for liberation. These disciples longed to give up their habit of objectifying self and other to trust in something bigger . . . and they were on fire. Their path expressed this, and we see that it paid off.

When we engage our spiritual discipline, we should have a plan, too. In fact, when we enter the path we are basically making arrangements for liberation. It's all very practical. How we decide to go about our liberation is individual. But we need vision: we need to know how the path works and how we will traverse it. We need support: teachers and examples. And then we need to give ourselves over to the process of change.

If we don't take command in this way, the only choices we have are to abdicate our discernment and hold the teacher and lineage responsible for our liberation—uh oh, blindism. Or conversely, relinquish our independence, in which case we may feel like the teacher and lineage are holding us captive—uh oh, doubtism. Questions might start to arise: Do I have to do everything the teacher asks? What if he asks me to do something I don't believe in? Do I have to agree with everything I read about in the texts?

Do we? Don't we? Should we? Shouldn't we? Life is not prescribed in this way. Relationships are not preplanned. We don't enter any relationship thinking, "I don't do windows," or "I'm going to jump off a cliff." What we will do, who we will be in the very next moment . . . we'll have to see. We'll have to rely on our own discernment, and it may surprise us.

The moral of these great meditators' stories is not whether or not we have to stick wood under our fingernails to attain enlightenment. The moral of their stories is that freedom requires us to trust our instincts for happiness. Freedom requires vision,

the supportive wisdom of the teachings, and independent thinking. It requires that we find the Middle Way beyond blindism and
doubtism. But most importantly, these stories raise a simple question: how will you attain liberation?

What's your plan?

21

To Walk by Faith

One morning as I was walking through Central Park in New York City, heading downtown and pondering the importance of faith, I saw a large church. Clinging to that church was an enormous purple banner with yellow letters that read, "For we walk by faith, not by sight."*

I'm not familiar with all the Christian interpretations of this quote. And I don't know what this meant to the person who said it. But it meant something to me.

When we live life as an open question, we get the information we need . . . sometimes even on a giant banner. Now whether that's life responding to our open question or whether we're just waking up to the world around us, I don't know. But I'm beginning to have faith that it happens that way.

WALKING BY SIGHT

Doesn't everyone want faith? What could be better? Faith makes life carefree, simple, and meaningful. Unfortunately, faith is not so easy to come by. That's because we walk by sight.

*2 Corinthians 5:7 (the words of Paul).

When we walk by sight we take things at face value, which means we let the world of appearances guide us. We rely on the whimsical and unfixable nature of things. Now by definition, can anything ambiguous, open to interpretation, moody, deceptive, or changeable be trusted? I don't think so. The best we can expect from the world of appearances is to manage it with anxiety, hope, and fear.

A dear passionate friend of mine, Juan Carlos, used to say that the teachings on the unreliable and boundaryless nature of things made him feel . . . groundless. Of course he was just voicing an experience we all had with the uncertainty of life. Juan Carlos—and hopefully the lot of us—has matured over the years. He has raised a family, watched his children grow, and gotten a good hit of life. I wouldn't say he's jaded; Juan Carlos has a lot of interest in life. But maturity comes from witnessing the unreliable nature of things—a lot of old age, sickness, death, and disappointment—and, most essentially, from realizing that there's nothing scarier or more "groundless" than relying on the unreliable.

Let's face it, we never know what happens next—we don't know what's on the other side—and the sooner we accept that reality, the better. And I don't mean just "face the facts." I think we can enjoy living this way, don't you? Curiosity, wonderment, amazement, and awe . . . we would have none of that if we already knew what happens next. We would have no "ahhh" or surprise. We'd lose the challenge of unscrambling our own personal mystery, we wouldn't grow, there would be no more open questions to ponder—no koans to play with. In fact, life would be inert. Would anyone want that? I doubt it. Better, then, to walk by faith.

WALKING BY FAITH

To walk by faith is like a supplication—a prayer. We supplicate when we don't know what to do, when through deep investigation we have given up hope in the unfixable world of things, when we know there's nowhere else to go. When we arrive at such a point, we find ourselves in a situation similar to that of the Buddha when he exhausted all views and sat with a wide-open mind beneath the Bodhi Tree. The Buddha's gesture of sitting beneath the Bodhi Tree in this viewless state was an appeal—a supplication to a bigger way of being.

Ordinarily, when we think of faith, we think of having faith in some thing. But that would be walking by sight, wouldn't it? So there's a twist here in the story of the Buddha. Through his example we learn that boundarylessness—this bigger way of being—is not some thing we can actually have faith in. It's not objectifiable or findable. It's not affirmable or deniable.

Faith is the mind of an open question. And when we ask an open question, we don't get some kind of static answer. We don't arrive at a final destination or reach a definite conclusion we can hold to and say, "That's it!" Faith is an experience, a way of being in life, that comes from a mind that does not reach conclusions about the world of things. So, in essence, to stay with this bigger way of being without turning away is what it means to walk by faith.

Perhaps you still think faith leaves you hanging in the balance. But if you keep at this practice, the practice of walking by faith, something may surprise you. As all the extraneous assumptions you have about the world—all the hopes and fears, all the exaggeration and denial—begin to fall away, you will encounter an unwavering certitude. This certitude is the wellspring of confidence, intelligence, and creativity, and it will sustain you. And, like the great beings of the past, present, and future, you will enjoy a fluid, vibrant, and dynamic partnership with the world.

Now, if this fullness of being is what you seek, in each moment ask yourself this: Can I stay present in the midst of limitless possibility? Can I relax with wonderment? Can I live my life as an open question?

Bibliography

Chandrakirti. *Introduction to the Middle Way.* With commentary by Jamgön Mipham. Translated by the Padmakara Translation Group. Boston: Shambhala Publications, 2002.

Changchub, Gyalwa, and Namkhai Nyingpo. *Lady of the Lotus-Born: The Life and Enlightenment of Yeshe Tsogyal.* Translated by the Padmakara Translation Group. Boston: Shambhala Publications, 1999.

Conze, Edward, trans. *The Perfection of Wisdom in Eight Thousand Lines and Its Verse Summary.* Bolinas, Calif.: Four Seasons Foundation, 1994.

Khen, Nyoshul. *A Marvelous Garland of Rare Gems: Biographies of Masters of Awareness in the Dzogchen Lineage.* Translated by Richard Barron. Junction City, Calif.: Padma Publishing, 2005.

Khyentse, Dilgo. *Enlightened Courage: An Explanation on the Atisha's Seven Points of Mind Training.* Translated by Padmakara Translation Group. Ithaca, N.Y.: Snow Lion Publications, 1993.

Kongtrül, Dzigar. *It's Up to You: The Practice of Self-Reflection on the Buddhist Path.* Boston: Shambhala Publications, 2005.

———. *Light Comes Through: Buddhist Teachings on Awakening to Our Natural Intelligence.* Boston: Shambhala Publications, 2008.

———. *Natural Vitality.* Crestone, Colo.: Sarasvati Publishing, 2007.

Kongtrül, Jamgon. *The Great Path of Awakening.* Translated by Ken McLeod. Boston: Shambhala Publications, 2005.

Milarepa. *The Life of Milarepa.* Translated by Lobsang P. Lhalungpa. London: Penguin Arkana Publications, 1992.

Nagarjuna. *The Root Stanzas on the Middle Way.* Translated by the Padmakara Translation Group. Dordogne, France: Éditions Padmakara, 2008.

Patrul Rinpoche. *The Words of My Perfect Teacher.* Translated by the Padmakara Translation Group. 2nd ed. Boston: Shambhala Publications, 1998.

Rabjam, Longchen. *The Precious Treasury of the Basic Space of Phenomena.* Translated by Richard Barron. Junction City, Calif.: Padma Publishing, 2001.

Saltman, Bethany. "Moral Combat: Chris Hedges on War, Faith, and Fundamentalism." *The Sun,* no. 396, December 2008. Interview with Chris Hedges.

Shantideva. *The Way of the Bodhisattva.* Translated by the Padmakara Translation Group. Boston: Shambhala Publications, 1997.

Shibayama, Zenkei. *The Gateless Barrier: Zen Comments on the Mumonkan.* Translated by Sumiko Kudo. Boston: Shambhala Publications, 1974.

Sumedho, Ajahn. *The Four Noble Truths.* Hertfordshire, U.K.: Amaravati Publications, 1992.

Thondup, Tulku. *Masters of Meditation and Miracles.* Boston: Shambhala Publications, 1996.